WE WILL BE BACK

SCARBOROUGH F.C.'S FAREWELL TO THE FOOTBALL LEAGUE

Ian Kerr

Aureus

First Published 2000

©2000 Ian Kerr
All photographs ©2000 Scarborough Evening News (01723) 363636

Ian Kerr has asserted the Author's right under the Copyright, Designs and Patents Act 1988 to be identified as Author of this Work.

All rights reserved. No part of this publication may be reproduced, stored in a retrieval system, or transmitted, in any form or by any means, electronic, mechanical, photocopying or otherwise, without the prior permission of Aureus Publishing.

Printed in Great Britain.

A catalogue record for this book is available from the British Library.

Aureus Publishing 24 Mafeking Road Cardiff CF23 5DQ.

ISBN 1 899750 68 1

Contents

	Foreword by Ian Kerr	v
	Foreword by Les Kershaw	vii
1	The Final Whistle blows	1
2	Scarborough are on their way to Wembley	12
3	Out with the old, in with the new?	24
4	Expectations are high!	31
5	Blast off!	40
6	Things can only get better	49
7	Who does own Scarborough Football Club?	56
8	Russell's return	62
9	No festive cheer	67
10	Wadsworth waves goodbye!	72
11	Too many chiefs, not enough indians	80
12	Hope springs eternal	88
13	Rock Bottom	94
14	No battle, no victory	104
15	The end of an era	115

Foreword by Ian Kerr

This book was written as a consequence of that fateful day Saturday 8th May, 1999. The day the World came to an end and the day in which so many loyal supporters of Scarborough wept tears of disbelief as we found ourselves void of Football League status.

Scarborough Football Club were the first Club to gain automatic promotion from the Conference League into the Football League in 1987. We remained there until the fifth month of the year 1999. We were relegated in the cruelest of fashions. A worst scenario you could not imagine. The last game of the Season. A goal scored by a goalkeeper. A goalkeeper who was signed after deadline day. A goal which ensured survival scored in the 96th minute. It doesn't bear believing!

Scarborough Football Club departed from the Football League having made so many friends in its time in the League. So many Clubs, and so many people expressed their sadness at our demise. We hope to make our stay in the Nationwide Conference, with all due respect, as brief as possible. We are here to visit, but not to stay.

8th May, 1999 was the worst day in the history of Scarborough Football Club. I have been at the Club for a long time, I have a deep love for the Club and all involved. I witnessed the incredibly sad emotions. The tears of despair shed on that Saturday, and, to allow such heartfelt emotion to disappear into the annals of time unsaid would have been unacceptable. This book was written as a testament to all loyal and caring people who share a burning affinity with their beloved Scarborough Football Club. This book is for you. 'WE WILL BE BACK'.

Ian Kerr

Foreword by Les Kershaw

The season 1998/1999 was a momentous year in the history of Manchester United Football Club. It was the season that we conquered Europe and won the double for the second time. It was also the first time that an English club had achieved the treble. It was a season that will be remembered for many, many years to come.

The season 1998/1999 was a momentous year in the history of Scarborough Football Club. For every Scarborough fan it will be a year they will remember for a long, long, time. Unlike United fans they will not remember the season with joy and pride but with sadness and disbelief.

It was the season when we were winning everything at the same time as Scarborough lost their treasured Football League status. They were relegated to the Nationwide Conference in the most unbelievable of circumstances. Anyone connected with football could not help but feel so sorry for that little club on the North East coast of England. After 12 years in the Football League they were relegated in the cruelest of ways.

I am pleased to lend my support to this book by Ian Kerr which catalogues Scarborough Football Club's last season in the Football League and follows the fortunes of my Club, Manchester United in our glorious season. I hope that Scarborough does as the book title suggests and gets back into the Football League. I hope they can regain their football league status as quickly as possible. I am sure that readers of this book will find it thoroughly enjoyable.

Les Kershaw
Academy Director
Manchester United Football Club

1

The Final Whistle blows

4.48 p.m. Saturday the 8th May, 1999. The incoming trawler, heavy with its catch, inched and bobbed, danced and weaved its way back into the South Bay, into the picturesque harbour of Scarborough. Back to its base. Ready to off-load its catch. The sea had been kind to her, a gentle swell and the presentation of an excellent catch of fish had been gifted to her. It had been a particularly fruitful sojourn. And, for its crew, they were more than ready to disperse to their homes and families. They had worked hard. It was a Saturday. It was the end of a long, hard week and they were more than ready for a well-deserved night on the tiles.

The little boy and girl, playing on the Southside sands, stopped building their magnificent sand castles to watch in awe at the sight of the little boat with a million dancing, singing seagulls hovering above its head like a thick cloud in a clear blue sky. They were mesmerised. They had come with their mum and dad that morning for a magical day by the seaside. The fishing boat and the singing, dancing seagulls added to the magic. It was a day they would remember for a long time.

The Brunswick Shopping Centre, in the heart of Scarborough, was steadily thinning itself out from the throngs of Saturday afternoon shoppers as they made their last purchases and headed home exhausted by their efforts to buy whatever they had come to buy. A new outfit. Or the latest Boyzone C. D... or, merely worn out by their ritualistic endeavours to buy nothing. It had been a good day for the local shopping fraternity. The

We will be back

town was busier than usual. There had been shoppers aplenty. Money was in their pockets to be spent and spend it they did.

Soon the town centre would clear. Temporarily. The 'shop 'til you drop' brigade would make their way home. The shop assistants, managers and owners would wave a welcome goodbye and gladly, hastily close up behind them. If the truth was known, relieved to see the back of them. Complete the day's business and follow shortly behind their customers and clients.

The town would not be quiet for long. The emptiness would disappear and the evening revellers would start to converge on the centre of the town like a swarm of locusts. This was Saturday night. This was Scarborough. And this is where it all happens. The town would throb with nightlife. Bars, pubs and clubs would all be bursting at the seams. The migrants had worked hard all week and tonight they would be out for a good time and tonight they would have a good time.

Heading out of town along Seamer Road on the A64 the traffic was bumper to bumper as they crawled, stopped and started, edged and pottered towards the outskirts of town. Seamer Road was always a traffic headache, today it was a motorist's nightmare. It wasn't a place for the chill out brigade. It wasn't a place for Mr. Cool. This was Mr. Angry's territory.

Roadworks had made the normally infuriating road into a road to hell. Grin and bear it was what any philosophical, happy motorist would resign himself to do. The road was not a haven for philosophers. It was the norm when roadworks cause delays. There were fidgeters, chain-smokers, cursers, oathing at anything and everything, from their poor ear-bashed wife at the side of them to the non-present Council road worker who had single-handedly created this chaos and who, if they could just lay their hands on him for a moment, a micro-second even, they would have his private parts taken from him and stuffed up his nostril! It was a place where road rage was just below the surface, eager to rise and cause mayhem, ike a volcano waiting to erupt.

There were little ones trapped in the rear of their dad's pride and joy tired and restless and just wanting to be at home where they could run free and create havoc in the sanctuary of their bedrooms. They couldn't understand why they were static. Why they were entrapped. They couldn't comprehend how their parents were blowing a fuse with each other. In the innocence of childhood they were doing everything they shouldn't. They couldn't grasp that silence and stillness would be the best order of the moment. Family cars, incarcerated in Seamer Road, were potential war zones.

Trapped in the mess were young boy racers with their latest, easily impressed, tasty piece beside them, fuming at the fact that Seamer Road roadworks had captured them. Stifled their style. And, that on another road, in another place they would be foot to the floor and driving as quick as the proverbial bat out of hell. Their bravado had firmly been put on the back-burner.

But here, there was no place to go, but sit in the mass and hopelessly try to dream up conversation. It was an impossible plight. Conversation is not the boy racers' strongest point. They had to suffer in silence. Their egos temporarily smashed in the immobile mess.

From the side streets, which linked on to the snail-paced travellers heading York-bound on Seamer Road, were motorists who had as much chance of joining onto and adding to the congestion as they had of having a burger on the Moon. No one, but no one already submerged in this motoring madness would give an inch. Smug grins, two fingers, silent f... offs were uttered in their direction, but caring car-driving courtesy was nowhere to be seen. They were trapped and no one gave a crap for courtesy!

Oblivious to the prisoners of the Road, a football match in the Nationwide 3rd Division had just finished. Yards from where they were incarcerated. Not just any football match. It was a match of vital importance. Yes there had been many other Football League fixtures played on Saturdays before at the McCain Stadium, Scarborough, but this was a match which meant much more. It was a game that meant so much to so many loyal, football crazy Seasiders.

In the stadium their beloved Scarborough had just fought out a 1-1 draw against promotion-seeking Peterborough. It was the last game of the Season. It was a game which would decide the Club's destiny. Their jubilant, joyous supporters leapt over the barriers and spilled onto the pitch happy in the knowledge that their heroes had taken seven points from their last three games. It could have been nine! Oh how it could have been nine.

They were singing and dancing and the echo of 'The Great Escape' echoed round the Stadium. Supporters danced the congo and hugged and kissed each other drunk in the satisfaction their team had finished ahead of their relegation, sacrificial lambs, Carlisle who were now doomed to the next Season in the Nationwide Conference and no longer members of the Football League. Or so they thought.

We will be back

As I disappeared up the tunnel and out of the sight of the celebrating army of supporters who had flooded onto the pitch, I sensed for the first time that something wasn't quite right. I started to drain of all the feelings of certainty I had earlier experienced. All those moments of total belief started to evaporate.

There was something in those chilling moments from the sound of the final whistle to entering into the changing area that was hard to explain. No more football would be played. No more points could be won or lost. Our Season was finally over, but there was no relief. Just an inner panic. Call it football intuition or paranormal but I still cannot explain the feeling that came over me. For the first time, belief turned to doubt.

Back in the depths of a freezing February when we were in the midst of a diabolical run of results, one win in nine, I remember having a one to one talk in the coaches' room with Ray McHale. Ray is Scarborough Football Club's Assistant Manager. He has been at the Club, off and on, since we came into the league back in 1987 and had witnessed all the highs and lows. He is Scarborough through and through. And we were now in the midst of an almighty low.

Ray is one of the most optimistic people I have ever met. His happy-go-lucky nature is infectious and he is frequently the man to pick you up when you are down. I call him Alka Seltzer. His effervescence has so often been the saviour of Club officials when there has been a confidence crisis. Some have had to be pulled back from the brink of suicide already this Season! Saved by Ray's optimism and belief.

During the conversation when we were talking about the Club's precarious position and the doubt that certain people had expressed I asked Ray, deep down did he have any fear that we would be the team to go down. Without any pause for thought Ray fired back he had no doubt we would survive and we would be playing in the third division next Season. I took great heart from that. Because, like Ray, I felt the same. I had no apprehension that we might be the team that takes its place in the Conference. I would be lying if I said there had not been evidence of doubt and despair at the Club, there had been. It was only natural. But I was completely confident we would live to fight another Season in the Football League and it was reassuring to hear someone else share in my belief.

Right up to that moment when the final whistle blew and the fans spilled over from the stands and terraces I had total belief, suddenly, in those short steps from the dugout to the tunnel something filled me with doubt. As we disappeared up the tunnel, the stewards ensured only those authorised, did so. The exuberant fans were halted by the crowd controllers. There was no problem they would just amass there and sing themselves hoarse until their heroes re-emerged.

In the Boardroom and Sponsors' Lounge the place seemed to be bursting at the seems. There were people wall to wall. The hierarchy of the Club and the selected clientele huddled together in corporate hospitality, hypnotised to the television in the corner. It was Saturday afternoon and the tele-printer was spitting out the results as it normally did, as they came in.

This was not uncommon. Saturday afternoon, post-match, the television would be on and the scores would be been relayed. Normally some people would watch and listen, some would watch and then talk, only hearing what they wanted to hear. The Manchester United score, the Leeds United result, others wouldn't pay any attention, more bothered about having the last ounce of corporate hospitality before they hit the road. Today was completely different. Everyone was engrossed. Everyone listened intently to every result, reacting as usual to certain teams' scores, but there was only one result they really wanted to hear. Carlisle hadn't won.

Manchester City 4 York City 0. There was a roar from around. The Seasiders arch-rivals had been relegated to Division Three. It was music to our fans' ears. We would be playing them next Season. Our closest rivals. Or would we? Please God please let us be playing them next year.

Cambridge 0 Brentford 1, Brentford had won the League. I didn't give a shit. We had taken four points off of the league Champions, it didn't matter a jot. Where was the score that would give us third Division salvation? What was the delay in the Carlisle score?

Other scores were given. Some of vital importance to others. This was the last day of the Season in the Nationwide Football League and there were major issues to be settled. That might have been, but none were more important than ours. There was a strangeness in these moments.

I couldn't see anyone else. The room was full but I was alone. Everyone was talking but I couldn't hear anyone speaking. It was an emotion I had never experienced before and likened it to when people have told the story of when they thought they had died and they had left their bodies and were looking down on things from above. It felt much like that. So weird.

Oblivious to the anxiety that was everywhere inside, outside, up above our heads, was the Chairman's wife Gillian and Trevor Milton, our vice-Chairman, poised in the Directors' Box, looking down on their flock, ready to uncork the champagne of celebration. They were just itching for

We will be back

*The Chairman's wife Gillian Russell waiting to uncork the champagne.
The bottle was never opened!*

those magic words that said Scarborough were staying up and Carlisle were going down. They were just willing the correct scoreline to be fed through to us that Carlisle had not got the result they so desperately wanted. The fans amassed below waiting, yearning to be soaked in the spray that would signal Scarborough were staying up. They would rejoice in the spray of success. That day the bottle remained uncorked!

As if transferred by time capsule, I somehow was back in our changing room, how I had got there I cannot recall, back with the players who had given their all only minutes before. The tele-printer was kicking out scorelines in the far corner. Like in the Sponsors Lounge before, every face was glued to the screen. There were crucial scores still coming in but they were totally insignificant to us. Every sentence uttered by the B.B.C. Presenter Steve Rider brought a gasp and then a sigh as it was not the result we all longed to hear. Where the flipping heck was the

Carlisle score. How on Earth had their score not come through. Surely we all hadn't missed it! This was not good for the old heart.

It was a changing room charged with emotion. Players' livelihoods depended on the outcome at Brunton Park. There were players suffering in silence. There were leaders keeping everyone under control. There were madmen damning the B.B.C. for not providing the score they wanted to hear. There was exasperation. There was anxiety. Nail biters now down to their knuckles. There was hope and belief, doubt and fear. Everyone waited, yearning for the result they wanted to hear. How I prayed for the result of salvation.

By this time, on any other normal match days certain players would already have been showered, dressed and making their way to the bar to have a desperately needed liquid refreshment. Not so today. Everyone was still exactly as they had been before the final whistle blew. Still in their kit, frozen in the moment. Not even a tie-up had been removed!

During the heat of our battle with Peterborough we heard the roar from our fans as word spread round the ground like a forest fire that Plymouth had taken a 1-0 lead. 'We're staying up, we're staying up Scarborough's staying up' resounded everywhere. Then, almost immediately after, our recent signing Darren Roberts was put through down the right hand side. Darren was in one on one with only the goalkeeper to beat. This was it, Darren was going to earn himself a place in Scarborough Football Club folklore. He would put us 2-1 up and the result at Carlisle would pale into insignificance. It wouldn't matter if they won 15-1!

Time seemed to stand still. Everyone seemed to be in a state of inanimation. Go on my son, let's hear that blissful sound when ball hits net. Rifle it into the top corner and make this man very happy. Send me into ecstasy. It didn't happen. The opportunity was missed and I didn't get the opportunity to lose myself in that magical moment of euphoria you only experience when your team scores a goal. That moment when your mind explodes with joy and nothing else matters in the World. When the ball is nestled in the back of the net and the referee is pointing to the centre circle. When Armageddon can be all around you but you are lost in the wonder of football.

Soon after, word was relayed to the bench that Carlisle had equalised. Nothing more. No further information was received. Please God let it be status quo in Carlisle. They can score goals on any other day, against any other side, but today shut up shop and let their game finish a draw. Let Carlisle be

We will be back

the team to experience life in the Nationwide Conference next Season.

Head hidden underneath my towel, concealing the torture that was etched on my face, I prayed and prayed begging for the result I wanted to hear. Pleading for the right to remain in the Football League. Hands ruffled my concealed head uttering words of optimism and re-assurance. Touching for the sake of touching and probably to alleviate their own personal anxiety and self doubt. I had been anticipating this day for months. I had discussed it a million times. I had re-assured hundreds of supporters they need not worry, everything would be alright and I had always informed anyone who asked that the victims of this terrible footballing crime would be Carlisle. There was no way my beloved Scarborough Football Club would go down. Their beloved Scarborough Football Club.

I knew how I would feel on this day if it went down to the wire. I had lived the moment a thousand times in the months and weeks leading up to this present time. At least I thought I knew how I would feel. I had no idea. There was absolutely no way I could possibly know that I would feel like this. I was experiencing a gut-ripping feeling the likes of which I had never, ever had the displeasure of feeling before and one which I hope I never undergo again.

Everything was hazed. Everything was spinning, turning, foggy. From the haze and the mist came the words which I prayed I would not hear. Steve Rider ripped through my towel and said 'We're getting news that Carlisle have scored a second goal.' The words hit me like a sledgehammer. Smashing in to my disbelieving skull. 'If that is right they will stay in Division Three and Scarborough will be relegated to the Conference.' 'No, please no, don't let it be...' 'Yes, it has been confirmed. Carlisle have scored a second goal. Scarborough will play in the Conference next Season. The final result at Carlisle is Carlisle United 2 Plymouth Argyle 1. Carlisle will remain in the Third Division next Season.'

Emotions crashed all round the changing room. A plethora of emotion. None affected me. Only my own. I lost the plot. I hadn't cried since my dear mother passed away nine years ago. Then, the tears didn't flow like they were falling today. I felt so guilty as I found myself crying more than I had when my beloved mother had taken her final rest.

Bill Shankly, the legendary Liverpool manager, had once said football is more important than life and death, this must have been what he meant. I kept repeating that it could not be. Please don't let it be true. It couldn't happen like this. It could and it did. And worse! How could it be worse?

The hero of the hour for Carlisle was their 'keeper Jimmy Glass. Glass had gone up for an all-or-nothing, last-gasp attempt to get the goal which would give Carlisle the goal, and the three points, and the win they required if it was to be Scarborough who were to make their Football League demise. Unbelievably, it was Glass that was to fire home the winner. In the fourth minute of injury time for God sake! The f...... Goalkeeper! This can't be happening! It was, and it did!

'He's the one they got after deadline day'. A muffled voice from the far corner of the dressing room uttered. I had forgotten this momentarily as I was lost in the tragedy of the moment. What had we done to deserve this? I had witnessed many incredible events in football before but this was something else. I don't know what the others were suffering within the walls of our home dressing room. I was cocooned in my own misery.

Tears flowed uncontrollably down my cheeks. I couldn't come to terms with the fact that it was us that would be lost from the Football League. People talk of the highs and lows of football. This had to be the lowest of the lows. Nothing but nothing could be any worse.

What would it mean to everything we had worked so hard towards? What did the future hold? Would there be no more 'glorious Chelsea nights'? The night we put the mighty Chelsea out of the Cup. All those memorable games when we caused major Cup upsets. What would happen to those young boys who we had just offered Professional contracts and were starting out in Professional Football? Would there be a way back to the Football League for them? Would they ever get the chance to play in the Football League? How would they be affected? God, please give them a chance to fulfil all their young dreams and ambitions.

The Chairman came in and from his many words of solace, which were lost to me in this living hell, I managed to pick out that the fans were outside and that they wanted to see the players and staff. They refused to be budged until they could share their sorrow with the players and management. They wanted to express their appreciation of the big, brave effort the players had put in in the last three games. Gallant but forlorn.

Today of all days, the presentation of the Club's player of the year, young player of the year and other awards were arranged to be presented. The presentation would take place in the McCain Lounge. It could have been the best day possible to have held the presentation if we had survived. As it turned out it couldn't have been a worse day to choose. Five of my young players were to receive a special award congratulating them on receiving their first Professional contract. Their careers obviously, immensely affected by our demotion. Their chance of Football League

We will be back

football may have gone before they have even been given the opportunity to start. To this day I have no idea who received Player of the Year!

Don't ask me how but I shuffled and staggered down the corridor past my boys, my young players whose futures were now hung out on the washing line, through the back-slapping, comforting supporters and up into the Directors Box. I tried to tell myself to control myself, maintain dignity and conduct myself sensibly. It didn't work. On seeing the Boro' faithful I broke down again. The tears were of pain and of sadness and worry of the future. Not just for myself but for the people who had put so much work into the Club. The Board, the management, the players. My youth team players, for the supporters and for the young players who were registered with our Club, their Club. Scarborough Football Club. The little ones who rushed home from School, grabbed a biscuit and their kit and raced to come for their weekly coaching. The lifeblood of

*Fans before our last game in the Football League
v Peterborough 8 May 1999*

the Club. Surely it could not be cut open and left to bleed away? Surely we could still ensure their footballing futures?

The worst day of my life. The worst day of so many others' lives. Scarborough Football Club had lost its Football League status. We were relegated. We would be competing in the Nationwide Conference next Season. Fact.

That Saturday night, as I left the Stadium I stopped for a few minutes, sat down alone in the East Stand and looked out onto the pitch. I reflected on our glorious years in the Football League. On some of the games that had been played here, some of the famous footballers who had graced their skill at the McCain Stadium and wondered if we would ever see them again. Surely we would see those days again?

I re-lived some of the magic moments that we had had. Big Lee Hirst's goal in the dying seconds to give us a three nil victory over Coventry in the Coca Cola Cup. The goal that gave us a 3-2 aggregate victory over them and took us, against all odds, into the next round of the Cup.

Darren Foreman's hat-trick against our arch-rivals York City. A beautiful display of finishing. The first hat-trick to be scored by a Boro' player in the Football League.

I reflected on the brilliant occasion just one year ago when we prepared to take on Torquay in the play-offs to earn the right to go to Wembley and play for promotion into the Second Division.

Many great moments came and went. Would they ever be seen again?

As I left the Stadium I'm not ashamed to say I cried again.

2

Scarborough are on their way to Wembley

MAY 1998

'Wembley, Wembley. We're the famous Seaside Army and we're going to Wembley. W E M B L E Y'. The final whistle had sounded. The relief. The joy. The satisfaction. What a beautiful feeling. The feeling of success.

The Diva Stadium, Chester. The travelling fans were singing their hearts out for the lads. They had done it. Forty six long, hard games in the Nationwide 3rd Division. It had been a long, arduous journey. Now we had arrived. The seadogs had done it. We had travelled the length and breadth of the country through rain and shine and we had conquered. We were worthy of our final league position.

Although it could so easily have been automatic promotion, we were in the play-offs having fought out a 1-1 draw with Chester. Our fourth draw in our last four league games. All that stood between us and the twin towers was two games against Torquay. Not a problem. We had only a few months previous smashed them 4-1 at the Theatre of Chips. It was merely a formality. Boro were on their way to Wembley.

The Seadogs would make their first ever appearance at our country's footballing Mecca as a Football League side. We were regular visitors in the 70's, as a Semi-professional side, but this was different. We were going to fight for the right to be promoted to Division Two. Next Season we would be playing at Maine Road. Manchester City against Scarborough that's more like an away fixture. Those Gallacher brothers would see the mighty Seadogs murder their beloved team. Kevin Keegan would be coming to the McCain Stadium with the multi-millionaires of Fulham. New grounds, new teams, new horizons. A new dawn beckoned.

As the fans dispersed from the Stadium on the journey back to Scarborough they were already pre-planning their trip to Torquay and a famous day at Wembley. They were going to celebrate like they had never celebrated before. Their heroes would see to that. All Season they had followed, albeit a few more of them today. They were up for it big time and a bit more too. 'Scarborough are on their way to Wembley' rolled off the tongue of every travelling supporter.

Back in the away changing room at the Diva Stadium, the players and management congratulated each other on their fantastic achievement. They had achieved the impossible in such a short space of time. Since the appointment of Mick Wadsworth we had risen from a team that had finished second bottom of the league on two consecutive occasions and Mick had taken us to the play-offs in two magical Seasons. These were the things that dreams were made of. Mick had promised success when he arrived and he had delivered. He was a man of his word.

The Chairman came in to express his appreciation and gratitude to everyone. He had been at the Club through many dark nights but at last he had got the rewards he had deserved for all his hard work, determination and sacrifice. He was a happy man and it showed. A man glowing with pride. A man beaming in the light of success.

It had been a tremendous Season, we had finished sixth, it could have been higher. We lost only once in our final thirteen games and we had played attractive, direct passing football that was appreciated by many and bemoaned by few. To some we were the best footballing side in the league. Not only this, the reserves had won Division Three of the Pontins League pushing the giants of Newcastle United into second place. Everything was now set for the play-offs. A very successful Season, but it was not over.

The final league table showed that Colchester United finished fourth on seventy four points, Torquay in fifth position also on seventy four points, but with an inferior goals- for record, the mighty Boro' in sixth place with seventy two points and Barnet in seventh place with seventy points.

The other play-off to determine who we would play and beat at Wembley was between Colchester United and Barnet. The first leg to be played in London. Colchester had come with a late run to finish fourth

We will be back

top. They were the team in form and they would be our likely opponents at Wembley. Yes, we were going to Wembley.

We didn't leave Chester until a few celebratory drinks had been imbibed. The players had earned a refreshment! The bar was a place where they could share their achievement, wallow in the magic of the moment and further forge the excellent team spirit we had at Scarborough. The jokers told their jokes. The piss-takers took the piss and everyone was happy. No one wanted the moment to end. They would still have been there now if they had been allowed.

The day was to be a long day. A day which nobody wanted to end. Everyone was immersed in the moment. The Club had come a long way and we all would take stock tomorrow, but today was a day we didn't want to end.

That night the town of Scarborough was filled with pride. Our little Club had given everyone an uplift. The bars and restaurants were filled with the conversation of the play-offs and Wembley. Everyone 'belonged.' Everyone was a supporter. The town was united in its pride of the Club. If you weren't a Scarborough fan out on the town that night, then you had to be an alien.

We all celebrated our success. Some more than others. But everyone celebrated. Proud of our achievement. The final table placings were there to be seen. We had all worked so hard and many a beer was swallowed into the wee, wee hours of Sunday morning.

It was eight days until the first leg at our place. Changes had to be made. Our old campaigner and battle-hardened midfielder Ian Snodin had been dismissed at the Diva. He would not take part in the final at Wembley. He would be missed, Ian was the type of player who could stop influential opponents from playing. Not just in that game, but forever.

In the hour leading up to games, watching Ian prepare for the match was like watching a scene from Doctor Jeckyll and Mr. Hyde. He would arrive at the ground, with his cheeky smile and infectious charm, conversing with all and showing why he is so popular with everyone. But, as the lead up to kick off approached the transformation in Ian was frightening. From Mr. Affable to Ivan the Terrible. Just before the referee would sound for the teams to go out Ian would be splashing water on his face and staring into the mirror with glazed eyes. The eyes of a madman. Ready to cause mayhem.

To say he was intimidating is a slight understatement. Ian was the Slobodan Milosevic of Scarborough. If a player needed wiping out Ian was your man. Ian wasn't just a destroyer, he could play too. He was the orchestrator of the team. He conducted the flow of the team. We knew he would be missed when we got to Wembley, but he would help us to thump Torquay.

Jason Rockett was about to take part in what would turn out to be his swansong in the Football League. May the 10th would be his penultimate game as a Professional Footballer. If Jason had been a horse he would have been taken to the knackers yard. His knees were gone. He was playing through the pain barrier and every game was a trip to the Dentist's chair. He was a warrior, a man you would want along side you in the trenches and he was prepared to risk his future well-being for the Scarborough cause. Jason was on his way to Wembley. He had been through the bad times with the Club and it would have taken a Kalashnikov bullet to stop him missing these good times.

Like every Club at this time of Season the treatment room was bursting at the seams. Our physio, John Murray was working his socks off to patch up the players. He knew he could do it. He had a week and a day to perform minor miracles, and minor miracles he performed. If there was a way there was a will with John.

John was very popular with the players and the brunt of many of their jokes. It is fair to say that John was not blessed with one of those cute little upturned noses that some handsome devils are born with. John had a nose that you could ski down. He would have been perfectly type-cast as Mr. Punch in Punch and Judy. And needless to say John's hooter was the recipient of regular tirades of abuse. Players frequently complained that the treatment room was too small to rehabilitate them due to John's nose being found everywhere. A regular rendition of 'Its here, its there, its every f...... where, Murray's nose' could be heard around the confines of the treatment room. John took all the jibes in good spirit and gave out more than his fair share.

The Commercial department worked frantically to provide the merchandise which would make the Club an extra few bucks and give the fans something they could cherish in the years ahead. Scarves, banners, shirts. You name it they would ensure we had it..... and a few more too.

Our Commercial Manager, Russ Green was one of those chaps who could sell sand to an Arab. He was a top banana. Very much one of the unsung heroes at the Club. He would work all hours God sent to ensure that every possible penny he could attract would be put into the Scarborough Football Club coffers. Russ's only problem was he was a fanatical

We will be back

Manchester City fan and life had not been kind to the City fans this year. The excuses he used to tender for their failings were heart-rendering. I used to hide from him on a Monday morning if City had lost as Russ's City sob-stories became more unbearable.

The Chairman, the Manager, the players were frequently found with a microphone stuck under their noses. 'Can you do it?' 'Will you be fit?' 'What does it mean to the Club?' and a thousand more questions. Every question answered with optimism. It was not a place for doubt, we were three games away from the Second Division. We had been over a decade in the third Division, it was time to taste the Second. It was time to move on up and bid farewell to the third division.

Everyone at the Club was working extremely hard to ensure they played their part in making sure Sunday the 10th would be a perfect day for the Club. It was a great time for everyone as they contributed to the moment.

In the lead up to the first leg it was a case of ticking over. The players were given days of rest and when they came in, sessions were light. A few shadow-play sessions and set plays. All the hard work had been done. All that remained was the demolition job on Torquay.

All Mick asked was for the players to maintain their focus, train, re-fuel sensibly and rest wisely. He knew he didn't need to tell them this, he knew they would do it. The camaraderie among the team in these lead up days was brilliant. There was a unity, a trust and a confidence in each other that they could see the job through. Everyone had a smile on their faces. Everyone was ready.

With each day that passed the big game drew nearer. And as the game drew closer the expectancy got greater. There was a buzz around the town. Football was the buzz word. Scarborough Football Club was on everyone's' lips. The McCain Stadium was the place to be on Sunday the 10th May. The local newspaper was filled with good luck messages from the businesses in town and the local radio stations were playing regular requests for the team. Whole families were planning a family day out at the Stadium on Sunday. Old folks homes had arranged for their residents to come and lend their support and the day could not come soon enough.

I remember sitting up in the Directors Box alone one hot, sunny afternoon, just me and my thoughts. We were only a matter of days away from the big one. There was a beautiful silence around the ground. She looked at her best. She could provide the surface for this year's World Cup final. Lush and crying out for football. The pitch was magnificent.

We will be back

I looked around the Stadium and proudly reflected on how far we had come. The two new stands which stand in all their splendour behind each goal, a far cry from the days when both home and away fans used to have to stand and endure the elements, creased up by the fierce North-Easterly Scarborough winds or drowned in a coastal deluge ruthless on anyone mad enough to stand in its downpour.

The Club had come a long way and I was so proud to be part of the moment. History was in our hands. We just need to grasp it and take it for all time. I said a little prayer in the stand that afternoon. It was probably the 300th prayer I had said since Chester but it was a special prayer. It was like praying at Lourdes or in St. Peters Square. I was praying in my place of worship.

On the day before the match I overheard two young boys in the town centre. One was dressed in an Arsenal kit and the other in a Newcastle kit. Both very much making it evident to anyone who came within their sight that they were true supporters of the teams that had earned the right to play at Wembley in the F. A. Cup Final. They were both saying that they would gladly see their Premier teams lose in the forthcoming F. A. Cup Final if it meant Scarborough being victorious over Torquay. I felt a big smile appear on my face at the words of those young Scarborians.

Walking through the town centre in those days prior to the big day was an experience. Everyone stopping and wishing you well. Everyone congratulating you in reaching the play-offs and everyone reassuring you that we would win and get to Wembley. Everyone informing you that they would be there cheering us on to victory. It was a lovely place to be.

Sunday 10th May arrived. It was carnival time. The Stadium found itself playing host to thousands of Scarborough fans it didn't know existed. Unfamiliar faces, 'fans' who couldn't tell you the difference between Jason Rockett and Stephenson's Rocket! It didn't matter, today they were Scarborough through and through. They may not have been at the Stadium since Hitler invaded Poland but today they were die-hard Boro' boys.

Everywhere was a sea of red and white. Little children with faces painted like a barber's pole, old men with wigs of shocking red, and disabled fans with wheelchairs bedecked in Scarborough colours. Today you had to be resplendent in your Boro' red.

Fans had been advised to arrive early. They did. The queue down Seamer Road was a joy to see. Men and women. Boys and girls. Wives and husbands. Fathers and Sons. Grandfathers. Grandmothers. Mothers and daughters. Generations of families. Today everyone was one big family of

We will be back

Scarborough supporters. The queue moved slowly but nobody cared. Everyone happy in the joy of the day.

The gates had opened early and the pre-match entertainment included local dance troupes and jazz bands. It was party time. There was a carnival atmosphere and the lead up to the game was enjoyed by everyone. Then the P. A. Announcer asked the fans to welcome onto the pitch Torquay United and Scarborough. The hairs on the back of my neck stood on edge. This was what it was all about. We were on the verge of making history. We were at the point of take off to another planet. The 2nd Division. A billion red and white balloons rose majestically into the mid-May sky as the two teams emerged onto the battle field. 'Micky Wadsworth's red and white army' boomed around the ground.

Young and old. Male and Female. They were one. Everyone stood and applauded their Red and White heroes. Even the quiet introvert didn't care who heard him as he shrieked his delight at the moment. This was one of those footballing moments when you could lose all your inhibitions and just go bananas. This was the moment everyone had been waiting for.

At last it was here. We could get the little insignificance of Torquay United out of the way and start preparing for a wonderful day at Wembley. We won the toss. We would be playing towards the screaming support of the home fans in the second half. This was the way we liked it. This was the way it was going to happen. The script had been written.

The game started like a hurricane with both teams steaming into each other. No quarter was asked. No quarter was given. It was not a place for the weak-hearted. Dwell on the ball and you got cemented. The football was not Brazilian. It was passionate. It was ferocious. It was blood and thunder. It was the Third Division play-offs.

Life seemed to be passing by at a thousand miles an hour. Everything was rapid and fuzzy. I remember looking at my watch and seeing the game was now into its 21st minute and thinking this is what they mean when they say 'time flies'. It must have been on Apollo 13 today! The game was end to end and it was only a matter of time before the deadlock would be broken.

Midway through the half the impossible happened, Torquay had the audacity to score. To spoil the party. Their striker Rodney Jack received the ball and like Roadrunner he was off, 'beep-beep'. The next thing we knew the ball was nestling in the back of our net. What had happened? This was not in the script. Okay it was a minor blip, dust ourselves down and lets turn them over. Our fans momentarily became a couple of thousand instant mutes. Silenced by the insult of Rodney Jack's boot.

The bench instantly commenced into analysing what had happened. Where had the goal originated from? Who lost possession? Who let the Roadrunner run? We should have kept the ball better. Our concentration was poor. All comments were thrown into the melting pot. Mick calmed things down again and said its gone. Just keep our shape and keep probing. He was right.

Yes!... shortly afterwards we got a penalty, up stepped Mr. Cool Gareth Williams, or was it Gareth Southgate? It didn't matter we still missed. Gareth had not struck the ball as well as he should have and it was comfortably saved by the Torquay 'keeper. Things were not going according to plan especially when Roadrunner went and did it again! 2-0 at half time. We were in a bit of a mess and we needed to make changes, our big Rolls Royce, Gary Bennett was suffering and would have to come off. We did not need this but changes had to be made.

Mick did what he is best at. He assessed, analysed and got into his players. We were struggling but we had been in this position before in the Season and we had overcome it. We could do it again. We had to have the belief and the desire. We had to be patient but take the game more to them. We had to play in their final third more and keep looking to create and take chances. This was no place for the weak-hearted. This was Dunkirk and we had to fight to win the battle. The players responded.

The second half started with a renewed spirit, a new sense of purpose, a higher tempo. We took the game to Torquay and after incessant pressure we scored. A corner on the right was met by a Jason Rockett power header. Jason got on the end of the cross as if his life depended on it. We were back in it. 'Come on Boro', Come on Boro', Come on Boro'.' The fans chanted.

It was a futile chant because before we could draw breath we conceded a third from a John Gittens header. It was over. We had been beaten 3-1 at home! We had let ourselves down, and all those fans who had come out of the cupboard were making there way back into it, chuntering their usual discontent. We had under-performed. We had shot ourselves in the foot. We should have been going to Torquay defending a comfortable lead but we were going to Somerset fighting for our lives.

Wait a minute. It was only half time. We could and would go down to Torquay and put the whole thing back into perspective. After all we had beaten them 4-1 before, we could do it again. We had only three days to dust ourselves down, pick ourselves up, and get back on the road

We will be back

Rodney Jack of Torquay who scored four goals in the Play-Offs against us. 10 May 1998

to Wembley. We had problems. Several of our key players would not make it, through injury or suspension. We were down to the bare bones and had a mountain to climb. Of Everest proportions.

The Torquay squad departed from the McCain Stadium after having a few refreshments in the McCain Lounge. They were very satisfied with their afternoon's work. They had worked extremely hard for each other and got the result they deserved. On their own admission, not the result they had expected. They would have been more than happy with a draw, so they would be making their way back to Somerset delighted with a very unexpected away victory, a 3-1 first leg win.

It was our intention to travel down to Torquay and stay overnight. This was what we intended to do in our preparation for the two games. However, plans were changed. We had been beaten at home and now we were going to travel down on the day of the second leg, stop off for a pre-match and then go and play the second leg at Plainmoor! I couldn't see Manchester United doing this. But this was the way it would be.

There was little time to reflect and take stock. The players were given the Monday off to recover. We met on the Tuesday and we went to Bramcote for a light training session. The atmosphere was positive and a few laughs could still be heard. It wasn't by any means all doom and gloom.

After training Mick went through the travelling arrangements with the players. He then went into a discussion with them. Any possible doubters could leave now. The twin towers could still be ours for the day. If you didn't believe it then Mick didn't need you. It was a discussion full of certainty. It was a discussion which left everyone feeling absolutely positive and convinced that we could still win on aggregate.

Wednesday the 13th. Unlucky for some but surely not for the Red and White Barmy Army. It was a beautiful May night on the English Riviera. We had brought a good following, many of our fans still had faith. In their hearts we were still going to Wembley. We were not. We got dumped 4-1. 7-2 on aggregate. Who would have believed it. Not me for sure. Rodney Jack had roasted us again and we could not deny Torquay were the team that deserved to grace the National Stadium. So close, yet a million miles away in the end.

The battle was over before we had got started. We again under-performed. We defended poorly and made some very costly simple mistakes. Added to this we finished the game with two sendings off and very much deflated. Our old war horse Jason Rockett had been our sole goalscorer again and this was to be Jason's last game in the Football League. There were more than a few tears shed that night in Torquay.

As we were ignominiously being eliminated from the play-offs, over in Scandinavia the Stamford Bridge supporters were on Cloud Nine, celebrating a magnificent European Cup Winners Cup Final win over the German team, Stuttgart. A brilliant goal from the little Italian wizard Gianfranco Zola, giving them their first taste of European glory, and their finest hour, in over twenty five years. A brilliant achievement for Chelsea. A brilliant achievement for British Football.

The 1997/1998 third division play off would be contested between Torquay United and Colchester United. The big day out at Wembley for us was not to be. All our hopes and aspirations of achieving promotion to the Second division via the twin towers had gone. The journey back to Scarborough, as you would expect, was a long, painful trip. It was a very subdued coach filled with little conversation but much reflection. What might have been!

It was back to Scarborough and back to business. There was to be no trip to Magaluf for our boys. They would not be going to the Costa 'Big Drinkies'. Whilst other less successful sides had taken their players over for an end of Season break it was not to be at Scarborough. Within a few days Mick Wadsworth had brought his squad together and done what every manager dreads, but has to do. Inform players who would be released. For those about to go it was clearly a very traumatic few days. They had gone so close to playing at the National Stadium and now were about to be told that they would have to start to find themselves a new Club. For some, maybe even find a new career.

Mick was clear in his mind. There was a big clear out. Before the next Season started, among others, we would be without Ian Snodin, Gary Bennett, Michael McIllhatton and Jason Rockett. Jason's career was over. He had been forced into retirement by chronic injury to his knees. He would be sorely missed. He had been a loyal servant and would walk through fire for Scarborough Football Club.

Many other players who had been involved in the highs of the 1997/1998 Season would not be part of the 1998/1999 Season. Would it be that maybe too much surgery was carried out too soon? Perhaps Mick only needed to fine tune things, allow the understanding and spirit another year to develop, and a few additions here and there to the team which had come so close. However, one of Mick's qualities was his decisiveness. If hard decisions had to be taken, Mick would unflinchingly take them. Mick had taken us this far. He knew what he was doing.

We will be back

With the players gone, some never to return, the management team tidied up the final pieces of the 1997/1998 Season. They could be proud of what the Club had achieved. They had worked tirelessly throughout the Season. Plans were laid down for the forthcoming Season and instruction was given to the administration staff to arrange fixtures for our pre-Season. They had worked diligently throughout the Season it was time to have a break and re-charge their batteries. Time for a well-earned rest.

The Season was over. It had been a very good Season. It could have been a brilliant one. We had come so close to making history for the Club but it was not to be. We had to be happy with making the play-offs. Progress had been swift. Mick had taken us from second bottom of the league to twelfth in his first Season. From 12th to the play-offs. It was rapid improvement. We could have so easily have gone automatically into the second division. This was something that would come back and haunt us in the Season ahead. So near, yet so far.

Mick Wadsworth and Staff at Torquay as we go out of the Play-Offs and lose our chance of a Wembley trip.
13 May 1998

3

Out with the old, in with the new?

SUMMARY 1998

The clear out had been incisive. Surprises, even shock, was expressed by some of the fans, and from people within the Club, but Mick knew what he was doing, after all he had not made many mistakes since his arrival. There would be fresh faces, a stronger resolve and next Season we would win the league. The close Season would be a hive of activity, or would it?

The Professional Footballers list of players being released, and receiving free transfers was always as thick as the Yellow Pages. This was a great start point for every manager. This is where the busy, enthusiastic manager could be found scouring the list to add to his playing staff for the forthcoming Season. Looking for that missing piece which would complete the jigsaw. That player who would bring him the glory he sought. The Championships. The Cups. Immortality.

The backbone to our team to be fair had gone. We had to look ahead to finding players who would provide the spine of the side in the 98/99 Season. Rockett, Bennett, Snodin and others would be difficult to replace, but replace we must if we were going to take the Club forward. If we were going to win the league. We were going to win the league!

There didn't seem to be a great deal occurring and there was an air of despondency around the town as the weeks passed and not much seemed to be happening. The fans had been promised progress. The

Club was on the up and changes would take place. Yes, players had been moved out but no new ones to take their place had moved in. What was causing the delay? Nothing was happening, the fans knew it would. But when?

We had made substantial progress over the last two Seasons, everyone yearned for further progress and we all wanted to take the Club forward, take it to new heights, make history. The foundations for the future are always laid during the close and pre-Season. We were clear in this and we had to ensure signings were made and strategies were put in place.

The domestic Season was behind us, but in France the big one was getting underway. World Cup '98. Could this be the year when England bring the trophy back home. Could this be the year when Scotland manage the impossible and progress to the second stage? Would one of the African Nations emerge as the first country outside Europe and South America to be crowned World Champions? Could this be the year when the boys from Brazil give someone else the chance to be Champions of the World?

It was a difficult period to get things done. We were back in looking to make progress but frustrated that we were unable to do so. Players we fancied to strengthen our side were uncontactable. Managers we wished to do business with were unobtainable. It seemed British Football had gone on its holidays. Maybe they were all across the Channel amidst the World Cup fever in France.

Glen Hoddle had taken over his squad under a cloud of disbelief. How could he have axed the mercurial skills of Paul Gascoigne. Okay, he was seen out on the town drunk as a monkey, devouring a khebab days before Hoddle was to announce his final twenty two, but surely Gazza could cause more problems to the World defences, even if he was a piss artist? Gazza, to some, even if blotto, was a better player than any of the other super-fit athletes Hoddle had chosen to select. We wanted flair not robots. The country was split by his decision. It was a very controversial but brave decision of Hoddle to make. Would he live to regret it?

World Cup mania soon took hold. England were quickly immersed in football hysteria. Gazza had not been missed. To many, Hoddle had been completely vindicated. The team opened in the Competition with flair and passion. The individuality of Gascoigne was forgotten amidst the flowing teamwork that England were displaying.

As the tournament took hold Hooliganism raised its ugly head once more. The English fans were to take the brunt of all that is bad in the game. Over fifty fans were arrested in Marseille. Many protesting their

We will be back

innocence, but all tarnished with the same brush as being mindless English Yobbos. Many, so unfairly.

In a pub in Paris, the Auld Alliance, Ally McCoist and a couple of friends had taken Ulrika ka ka Johnson to have a drink with some of the tartan Army. Allegedly, Stan Collymore was to have come in to the bar to ask Ulrika to leave with him. She didn't want to do so. Stan ended up with a pint of beer over his head, kindly donated by some jovial Jock, and, amidst his anger he attacked and injured the lovely Swedish Television presenter. It caused a storm of protest back home, and Stan would have to suffer for his scandalous behaviour. He had inflicted serious wounds to his lovely girlfriend of the time. The Season ahead would be a complete non-starter for Stan.

On the pitch, England had showed flashes of brilliance, but stuttered on the back of a late defeat to Romania, to reach the last 16 and faced the might of Argentina in St. Etienne. The Argies had looked brilliant in their opening phase. This was going to be tough but it gave England the opportunity to finally pay back Diego Maradona and Argentina, after 12 long years, for the 'hand of God' goal. The goal that ended their dream in Mexico in 1986. This would be their day of deliverance.

The build up to the game was electric. Two nations who were not only football adversaries but two nations who opposed each other in war over the Falkland Islands. The media had a field day. The hype that surrounded

Jason Rockett - Scarborough's defensive stalwart

the game was passionate. Things had politically got a little better between the two countries but this was a game both desperately wanted to win. For football and for politics.

The game lived up to all expectations. It had everything. From the first minute both teams went at each other by the throat. It was, if not the game of the tournament, it certainly was one of the best games of the competition. The game was played at a fierce tempo with end to end committed football. It was evident this was not going to be a boring 0-0. There were clearly going to be goals and the approach was; the best form of defence is attack. It wasn't long before the first goal was scored.

The ball broke down the Argentinian left hand side. Ortega cleverly took it past Seaman and was brought down by the England 'keeper. Penalty and 1-0 to the South Americans. A debatable penalty to say the least. Not long after it was England's turn. Michael Owen burst into the Argentinian penalty area to be fouled and the referee instantly pointed to the spot. Shearer strolled up and in his usual confident manner fired the equaliser.

Each side's first goal came by way of dubious penalty decisions. I have to say I don't think either was justifiable. I think the attacking players were inviting contact to be made on them and reacting dramatically to any contact.

One of the great negatives of the 1998 World Cup was the frequent 'diving' that was evident, and this needs to be eradicated quickly from the game before the cancer spreads. Players were falling over like there was no tomorrow. There were several players out there who could dive better than Mark Spitz! If we are not careful coaches may find themselves coaching children in the art of diving in future coaching sessions!

Although there was instances of football theatrics the game was still brilliant to watch. Great pieces of skill, fast, flowing football and two very gifted sides not prepared to sit back and invite pressure. It remained at 1-1 for what seemed a short while.

Then late in the first half Michael Owen had five majestic touches on the ball. Control, direction, pace, power and clinical finish. Michael Owen suddenly became the King of England. A wonder goal, to grace the best stage in the World. The eighteen year old became a sudden super-hero. England were ahead. Briefly. The Argentinians got a debatable free kick on the edge of the box, but the cleverness of their set play was a joy to watch as they carved out a brilliant equaliser. They left the English defence stunned by their innovativeness. Another goal out of the top drawer. It was now 2-2 and anyone's game.

We will be back

At half time the television studios were drooling over the magic of Owen. This had to be the goal of the tournament. It rivalled Maradona's against England in Mexico. It was the goal which would shoot Michael Owen into superstardom. This goal was going to go down as one of the best goals ever seen in the World Cup. Michael magic.

The Nation held its breath. England had performed excellently and were looking as if they could exploit the Argentinian defence in the second half. They looked the side that could go on and claim victory and take a step nearer to becoming the footballing champions of the World. There was nothing to fear.

Shortly after the second half began, after a less than fair tackle on him, David Beckham did the unthinkable. He let himself, his team and the Nation down by a foolish piece of misbehaviour. David would have this act of stupidity rammed down his throat by every opposing fan in the country in the months ahead. To some, he had betrayed his country. David would have to be strong in the Season ahead to deal with the tirades of abuse that would be thrown his way. He was rightly shown the red card for retaliating on the Argentinian who had only moments earlier pole-axed him.

England gallantly held out through normal and injury time. Coming so close to actually winning it in normal time. Every man a hero. Every English player giving his all. Then, the dreaded sudden death penalties put them out of their third major competition, in the nineties. Such a terrible way to bid your farewells, but it was the end of the road for the valiant English. Batty adding his name to the illustrious names of English penalty criminals, Pearce, Waddle and Southgate.

Scotland performed bravely but it was Au Revoir as usual at the first phase. They had battled, rattled and raised hopes only for them to commit suicide again, against the Morrocans. The tartan Army were everyone's favourites again. They had been a credit to their Nation as they danced and drank their way through the football festival in France. Bravehearts to the end.

During World Cup fever the McCain Stadium had not been a hive of activity. The flow of fresh legs had not materialised. It was a difficult close Season for the Club. The Chairman had worked miracles in the short time he had been at the Club. The Stadium had a complete facelift. It was now one of the best Stadiums in the league. He had brought respectability to the town and he had put his hard-earned money where his mouth was. It had taken its toll and he was feeling the strain. He was ready to pass the reins over to someone else. Someone who could give the Club a new impetus. Someone who could take the Club forward. Someone who could inject the much needed money to invest in new players and bring the Club the glory the fans yearned for.

Scarborough Football Club is a small, family-friendly Club. Poorly supported but passionately supported by the chosen few. Everyone at the Club does their job for the love of the Club not for the hope of making themselves a fast buck. Fast bucks have never been found down Seamer Road. The work carried out behind the scenes is often unrecognised, rarely rewarded, but nonetheless never shirked. If the ground needs a fresh lick of paint, or the terraces need weeding then samaritans will appear. Life in the 'hard shoulder' of football may be a life of penny-pinching but it is a life of love and loyalty and care.

The Stadium had come a long way, in a short space of time. Since the Justice Taylor Report the transformation has been swift. Two new stands have been put in place behind each goal. The Shed running alongside the far side of the pitch has been re-roofed. The sight where that crazy Wolves supporter had fallen through in our first ever game in the Football League, was no longer evident. The Shed looked brand new, and the terraces have been greatly improved. Above all, the quality of the playing surface has been improved beyond recognition. This Season the players would have the opportunity to play on a surface which had not been seen at the McCain Stadium ever before. The ground staff had worked intensely throughout the months before and could take great pride in what they had produced. It was like a lush bowling green. The Stadium was a sight we all could be proud of.

July was upon us and pre-Season was due to commence. Amongst other trivial things, the training kit had not arrived! Surely this didn't happen at Old Trafford? Surely Ryan Giggs didn't return from his jollies to be told he would be wearing last year's left-overs? This was Scarborough Football Club and that was what was about to happen.

To say Mick Wadsworth was a little perplexed was like saying Hitler was a bit of a naughty boy. He was livid. He was a thorough man, very meticulous, who liked everything to be done yesterday and couldn't come to terms with people who couldn't match up to his high standards. He often would say 'Don't tell me why you can't do it. Tell me how you can!'

To say our Commercial Manager was running about like a cat on hot cinders was not an understatement. He was frantic trying to ensure that when the players arrived they would be beautifully kitted out in our new

We will be back

Club training kit and oblivious to the fact that he had nearly had a cardiac arrest flying here, there and everywhere to get it. But get it he did, and oblivious the players remained!

The draw for the Worthington Cup had been made and we would face last year's favourite Premier scapegoats, Barnsley. It was a good draw. Barnsley being our South Yorkshire neighbours, and would hopefully provide us with a sizeable crowd and a decent gate receipt.

We had previously had some great Cup wins and runs in this Competition and we were hopeful this year would give us the opportunity to achieve some further glory and some vital finance for the Club. Barnsley, after all was a Yorkshire Club and no doubt they would bring a big following to the East Coast. A welcomed following.

A good run in one of the major Cup competitions can mean so much to a small Club like ours. It can generate massive revenue. One big game against the likes of Newcastle or Manchester United could almost bring in more money in one game than all our home league games in a Season. It can put the Club on the map and it provides small Clubs with the opportunity to show the bigger Clubs some of the young talent they have on their books. Not to mention the money that can be found from television rights if you are lucky enough to find Sky wanting to televise your tie. Oh! how everyone wished for a great run in the Cups and to be drawn against one of the Premier League glamour sides.

At last the fans were starting to here that new faces were to be seen at the McCain Stadium. We had taken Ian Milbourne from Newcastle United on a free transfer. Quickly issued with the nickname 'Jackie' for obvious reasons. Paddy Atkinson had arrived from our old foes York City. Wayne Bullimore a cultured midfield player had pledged his footballing future to Boro' along with Jason Lydiate a Centre Back from Blackpool and to complete the line up of fresh faces we had gone European and brought Alex Marinkov from France.

Alex had not been in the World Cup winning squad but he would be our new Frank Lebeouf! Mick had not received the money he was relying on to take the Club forward. The Chairman didn't have the money to give him but we were set for the new Season. Everyone was optimistic. We had come so close last Season. This Season we would take it on a level and not be subjected to the uncertainty of the play-offs. We were going route one to Division Two. A finish in the top three. This time it would be automatic promotion.

4

Expectations are high!

PRE-SEASON 1998/1999

The Holiday Season was underway but it was like the proverbial damp squib. Unlike the Summer of '97 this Summer had about as much Sun as Iceland in November. It had been dismal. The odd glimpse of the current bun was quickly superseded by days of torrential rain. Consequently business for the local hoteliers, publicans and ice cream vendors was dire.

The business fraternity were pleading for a change in their fortunes. All they wanted was weather conditions similar to the Ghobi Desert for the next three months and for the town to be overrun by a glut of holiday makers with the same spending power as the Sultan of Brunei. It wasn't much to ask. They depended on long, hot Summers, so why were they getting weather conditions suitable for canoes?

Like many other attractive places to visit in Britain, they become less appealing to the visitor when they find themselves soaked to the skin, shivering in Summer and thoroughly cheesed-off. Scarborough had put together their pre-Season programme. It was the usual intense period of condition training, recovery periods and a programme of games in preparation for August the 8th and Southend at home. The preparation had been thorough and planned meticulously towards the opening day of the Season and lift off.

There was no tour of the Orient for us. Not even Leyton Orient! We would not be brushing up our match fitness in South Africa against Ajax or Inter Milan in some glamorous, if meaningless competition. We would not be invited to play in the unofficial Club championship of the World. In some far off exotic place with the guarantee of one million pounds for bringing the team and a further million if we win the four team tournament!

It was a little less glamorous for us. We would open with a visit to Whitby and then progress to a four team tournament in York, not New York, but 40 miles up the road to play against Barnsley and Airdrie and York City. No danger of our players suffering from jet lag or going down with malaria. Passports were not an essential accessory.

We would then play amongst others Manchester City and finish up our build up to 'D' Day with a visit from one of our most famous ex-managers, Neil Warnock and his team from Bury. And finally a trip from the mighty Newcastle United. The beaten F. A. Cup finalists.

The Club was now under new Chairmanship. Ken Ferrie had taken over the head of the ship from John Russell. Ken was a prudent Scot. A local businessman in the town who was on the board prior to taking up his new role and apparent of the financial plight of the Club. Ken was an honourable man. Honest and fair and not afraid to say no. He felt he had to say no. If the Club was to stay in existence then tough decisions would have to be made and people would have to accept that we did not have an endless flow of money to continue to say yes to every request.

Ken had been invited to a forum at the Stephen Joseph Theatre in the Round and stated that last year's big push had cost a large amount of money, money which the Club could ill-afford, and money which had now left the Club in financial difficulties. Hence the lack of cash for Mick to invest in new players. Purse strings had to be tightened. The survival of the Club depended on it. We could not afford to push the boat out at the risk of losing everything we had worked so hard to achieve. Or could we?

The Club had just taken on its new intake of young footballers on a three year Soccer Scholarship Programme. These were young boys who had just left school and were starting out on the long and arduous road to Professional Football. They were also easy prey for the practical jokers at the Club. Still a little green behind the ears. Having just left school and still a little naive towards the mickey-takers of the football world.

This year Adidas were committed to providing a package of their brand of sportswear to every trainee on the Soccer Scholarship Programme, and a magnificent package at that. Every boy would receive boots, indoor training shoes, tracksuits, sweat tops, towels, wash bag, flip flops, you name it,

We will be back

Adidas were supplying it. It was a brilliant deal for the boys. Previous trainees were used to receiving last year's left overs. This was slightly upmarket. But there was a price to pay for this enviable package, at the expense of the pranksters.

On the day the boys received this wonderful delivery of textiles and footwear Ray McHale informed the boys that the local press would be attending to get a photograph of them receiving their new Adidas sportswear. Ray was telling a tiny porky. Ray told the boys it would make an excellent photograph if the boys would don different parts of the Adidas gear and that the photograph would be best taken outside the main gates of the McCain Stadium.

Now, outside the main gates of the McCain Stadium is Seamer Road. One of the only roads into Scarborough. And one of the busiest. It was a hot July morning and the road was very slow moving with motorists bumper to bumper, heading into town. Unaware that there was about to be some cabaret outside the McCain Stadium.

We suggested one of the boys get undressed and wrap his Adidas towel round him and put on his Adidas flip flops. Another boy was to wear only his underpants but strategically place his Adidas holdall over his midrift and on his feet he was wearing the latest Adidas Predator boots. One boy was in his Adidas shorts and baseball cap and he was to hold a tin of Adidas Deodorant under his arm pits as if to be spraying himself. They were all very obliging in ensuring we got the best photograph for the local press and for Adidas.

The only thing that was concerning them was that, as they stood there striking their best modelling pose, the photographer hadn't arrived! Where could he be? We left them outside the ground, very concerned about the absence of the papparazi and went to ring the local press to enquire why there was such a delay! The boys were outside for about half an hour and attracted much attention from the day trippers and passers by! To this day the photographer never showed!

One of the first things Mick Wadsworth did on his arrival to the Club was to look at the training facilities used by the Club. One of the first things he did was to instantly improve them. Until Mick's appointment the Club had accepted sub-standard training surfaces. This would change. He was only prepared to accept the best and what he found by way of the training facilities at Scarborough and where he would lay down his training methods and tactics was not good enough for him. They had to be improved. If he wanted passing football played on the floor then the surface had to be suitable to do so.

We will be back

Mick quickly set about finding better facilities, facilities suitable for a Football League Club, not a Sunday League side. With his power of persuasion Mick acquired the use of a local private School's playing fields. They were much more appropriate. The playing surface was excellent. It was enclosed and allowed the team to train without the problem of interruption from the public. This is where the vast majority of pre-Season training would take place.

Needless to say, the Private School is largely attended by children from rather well-to-do families. Common christian names such as Tobias, Tristan and Quentin are to be found at the School. Children who think the word damn uttered by a human being should result in them having their mouths washed out with soap and water. Lovely, lovely children, but children who were rather unfamiliar with footballing banter.

Mick had to express to the players that guttural language had to be prohibited. Especially if the children were out enjoying the solace of a break time from lessons. This was about as easy as asking the players if the would kindly converse in Egyptian. 'Flip' is not the easiest thing for a footballer to utter when he misses the target from six yards and gets a set of six studs down his shin in the process. We had a lot of laughs as we hopelessly tried to put on our 'Sunday best' language.

The players returned in early July after their Summer vacation. This was usually a time when some unbelievable stories were to be told. Yes, some had gone for a quiet family holiday to the Costa Plenty. Others had a romantic fortnight on the Greek Islands with their girlfriends. Even threatening to marry them! And then there were others who had created bedlam in Benidorm and mayhem in Magaluf!

One of the players had apparently not seen one ray of sunshine in his two weeks there. It wasn't that the sun didn't shine, it was just he didn't see it. He was nocturnal for fourteen days. He slept through the day and went out to play in the evening!

Another, didn't know where he had been. He could have spent a fortnight on Mars for all he knew. He knew it was a place called Alcudia. He knew it was hot, but he had no idea where it was! The usual tales of waking up to find they had no eyebrows or one side of their hair had been shaved off were told. There was even one story where one of the player's friends had put capsicum in his Sun Tan lotion!

To be fair to the players everyone returned showing a good level of fitness. They had clearly been doing their maintenance fitness through the close Season. The days of players returning looking like Cyril Smith and moving like a pregnant sloth have long gone. They were back looking lean, mean and ready to go.

Training was intense. Mick always demanded quality on the training ground. It was not the place for jokers and easy riders. Aches and pains, bumps and bruises, pulls and tweaks reared their ugly heads, as is commonplace at the beginning of a new Season. Mick barked out greater effort in those early days. The players barked out what a twat he was!

Mick was very much one for getting players fit through games. Conditioned and Invasive games were prominent in these first few days interspersed with Interval aerobic work and sprint repetitions. Double sessions. The players would work hard in the mornings, return to the Stadium, where a meal was provided and then return for another Session in the afternoon. It wasn't uncommon for some of the players to see their meal reappear in the afternoon!

As the first week of pre-Season drew to a close and the players had a few days to recuperate they could sit back and relax over the weekend as the World Cup Final took place. Perhaps dream of there chance of one day playing in the biggest game that football has to offer. The hosts France would do battle with the invincible Brazilians. The whole World would be watching but everyone knew it would be a formality for the Samba Boys.

The third and fourth place play off had taken place just a few days before and, as usual, it had as much significance as news of a horse being born with four legs! Already some people had forgotten which teams were involved. It must surely be one of the most difficult games for a footballer to motivate himself for. Only days before he had just missed out on the opportunity to play in the biggest game of a footballer's life, with the whole world watching. And only days later he would have to suffer watching the experience unfold in front of him, without him being involved. The teams? The score? I forget!

Before kick off there was complete panic as news filtered through that Ronaldo might not start. For goodness sake. The World's greatest footballer. How could they not play Ronaldo! All sorts of reasons were transmitted. Ronaldo had taken very ill. He was injured. His girlfriend had left him. To an accusation that his sponsors were preventing him from playing. What a commotion, what a farce.

Ronaldo made it. After all the hype and doubt. He was in the team, but he might as well have not been there. He had a holocaust. As my old father used to say. He got one kick of the ball. It was a header and he missed it! The French totally dominated a pale, insignificant Brazilian side

We will be back

and became the Masters of Football in their own back yard. Vive la France.

The streets of France were awash in the tricolors. It seemed every French man and woman were out celebrating their country's miraculous victory, and rightly so. The French team had won the most prestigious trophy to be won in football. They had won it in their homeland and they had won it with a brand of football which was a pleasure to watch. The boulevards would be bouncing long into the night.

The World Cup was over. What a great competition it had been and soon some of those magical stars who had set the big stage alight would be winging their way over to England and the Premiership to display their talents to the English fans. The finest players would get a small period of rest before having to resume and prepare for another hectic, very demanding Season ahead. The rewards may be vast but the effort to achieve at the highest level is gruelling.

Scarborough would not be one of the teams to join in the World Cup transfer market. Ronaldo could stay at Inter for all we cared. Zidane was not needed at the McCain Stadium and Rivaldo could stay at the Neau Camp. We were happy with our group of players and besides the mighty Boro' didn't need them!

It was reported in the news at this time that there was chaos in the medical profession. The wonder drug Viagra which had hit the market only a few months earlier had not hit as hard as they had envisaged. Supply was far exceeding demand. 'Patients do not want as much sex as we imagined' said one leading, prominent medical spokesman! Is he sure? Maybe the problem of impotence was not as great as they had first feared, or as some joker said, too many people were having difficulty swallowing it, getting it stuck in their throat and developing a stiff neck!

As we approached our opening game of the Season against our seaside neighbours Whitby, players were looking sharp, but did we have the quality, the grit and the experience of the previous, successful Season? Did we have the strength in depth to fulfil our intentions of promotion to Division Two? Players can look excellent on the training ground but can they perform where it counts, in matches?

It was very early days but we would get an indication over the forthcoming weeks if we were to mount a charge for the Division Three title. If this largely, newly assembled squad of players had what it takes to stay at the summit of the Third Division. The future would reveal all.

In our opening game at Whitby we got smacked 3-0 and were lucky to get nil on the night. It was not one of our best performances and we made some elementary mistakes in defence and had about as many chances to score as a monk on a desert island! We were disappointing to say the least, but what did it matter. It was purely an exercise to work towards match fitness and build team shape. No need to go overboard and panic.

The next day it was as if we had lost the World Cup Final in the last minute as some people went O.T.T. about the team's lacklustre performance. How could a team like Scarborough get humiliated by a team like Whitby? What had caused this calamity? It happens all the time in pre-Season. Even in Season. Just swallow a chill pill and put it into perspective was the order of the day. We had gone up the North East coast and got licked but in terms of importance of the result it was absolutely minuscule. Lessons had to be learned but that's the nature of a pre-Season.

The Club had officially been put up for sale. It needed a new injection of ideas, expertise and money. The Russell regime had taken the Club a long way forward and were ready to take life a little easier, a little slower. They had been working tirelessly with little reward for their hard work and dedication. It was time for a new leader.

In our next run out we travelled to Bootham Crescent to play in a four team tournament at York. Again there was no need for altitude training for this trip. It was a short journey down the A64. Passports would be surplus to requirements and we would not need to cross through any time zones! We were drawn against Barnsley, our Worthington Cup opponents in a month's time and York, the hosts, were drawn against Airdrieonians. Surprisingly, SKY decided not to cover this major tournament!

This was more like it. We started with a good win over, it must be said, a very young, inexperienced Barnsley side. But, any win is a good win. We won 1-0 and played Airdrie on the Sunday in the final. This was a real crowd pleaser with goals rattling in from everywhere. It finished 4-4 and we won by way of penalties. It was a good confidence building weekend and one which we could take heart from.

The following week we lost Ian Snodin to Doncaster Rovers. There had been much speculation that Doncaster wanted their famous prodigal sons Ian and Glynn to return and guide the Rovers back into the Football League. It was without doubt Doncaster's gain and our loss.

Doncaster had not been in their healthiest of states and the people of the town had been canvassing for Ian and Glynn to take over and put the Club and the town back on the football map. They were Doncaster boys who had done good in their playing days and they were two people revered by the people of Doncaster. The Club made the correct decision and put Ian in place, and the man responsible for bringing glory days back to the Racecourse.

Ian was an out and out winner. He was a leader on the field and would be much missed by some of the young players Mick had brought in. But as Ian moved out Mick replaced him with Jamie Hoyland. Jamie was to come in as player/coach and provide the Club with the experience and leadership which Ian had given before him. It was not long before Ian was joined by his brother Glynn to form the new management team at Doncaster. Everyone at Scarborough wished them well, we all knew how tough life would be in the Conference!

News circulated around the Club, and in the town that the sale of the Club was imminent. It soon transpired that the new owner would be Anton Johnson. This set the odd alarm bells ringing around the town. Anton did not have a good track record in his dealings with Football Clubs and there was much apprehension to be found in the town. Reassurances were provided that Anton was buying the Club with the best of intentions and that there was money to spend. 'Money can buy success' Anton stated to the fans who wanted to hear those kind of words.

During this month there was an abundance of managerial change occurring in the leagues. Among others, Walter Smith left Glasgow Rangers after winning absolutely everything there is to win in Scottish football to join Everton. Steve Bruce joined Sheffield United in his first managerial role after winning everything there was to win as a player at Manchester United and Gerard Houllier became joint manager of Liverpool with Roy Evans! A strange appointment and one which everyone says is doomed before it starts.

In our next two games in preparation for the new Season we were roasted at home to a very impressive Manchester City. I thought on that viewing alone they would win automatic promotion. Their passing and movement was impressive and there was a good end product. Their finishing was clinical. We were clearly second best on the night and went down 4-1. This was followed by another home defeat at the hands of Bury.

At this time, it was reported that our home midweek matches would now be played on Wednesday evenings as it was felt that we would receive better support on Wednesdays than we had done on last Season's Tuesday evening fixtures. This might have been the case if Alex Ferguson's Manchester United hadn't been so flipping brilliant in Europe!

Every time we seemed to be playing at home, on wet, windy wintry nights, in those big, attraction games against some of the elite of Europe, like Darlington or Leyton Orient, United would be on the telly playing

Inter Milan or Juventus! This caused only a minor problem to a Club who found it difficult enough to attract the locals to support their home town team. Come and get frost bite at the McCain Stadium or sit at home, with a nice glass of wine and watch United in Europe by a lovely warm fire! Not a difficult choice. I think next Season we should play our midweek matches on a Sunday morning!

The pre-Season programme was almost complete. Training had gone smoothly. Mick was confident and although we looked rusty and a little unsmooth on occasion he was sure we were ready to meet the challenge of our opening game with Southend United. He was quoted in the press as saying the play-offs were a realistic aim. Time would tell.

The completion of the take over of the Club would be made on the opening game of the Season. Anton Johnson would buy 51% of the shares in the Club and the future running of the Club would be dealt with by Anton and his Company. The Russells would stand down after four years at the helm of the ship.

Just as pre-Season was about to finish and the acid test begin we were all shocked to the foundations when we were informed that Ray had a cancerous growth in his neck. Ray had never had a day of illness in his life and suddenly he was hit for six with this terrible news.

One day after training, as we were about to sit down to lunch, Ray noticed he had developed a lump on his throat. Mick had suggested it might be a wasp sting! Our physiotherapist referred Ray immediately to a doctor to diagnose the problem. Ray was informed it was cancer of the lymph gland and would require it to be removed. Within days this had been done, and not long after Ray had a second operation to have the other removed. It was a time of great concern for everyone, not least of all Ray and his family.

The new Season was knocking at the door. The fans were expectant. We had come a long way and they wanted more. Last year's achievement had whetted their appetites. They wanted to taste success. They wanted to witness history in their lifetimes. They wanted Boro' to make a surge into the second Division. It was that time of year when all teams are equal. Every fan is optimistic and football supporters' wives are eagerly awaiting the sanctuary of Saturday afternoons when they can escape the persistent chirpings of their football fanatical husbands. The first whistle was about to be blown. The first kick off was about to be taken. Would this be the year of the Seadogs? Would the last full Season before the new Millennium be historical for Scarborough Football Club?

5

Blast off!

AUGUST 1998

THE 1998/99 SEASON KICKS OFF

At last, the wait was over. The 8th August beckoned the first day of the new Season. The opening Saturday is unlike any other Saturday, it's unique in the football fans' calendar. Those empty, worthless Summer months when Saturdays seemed so boring and football fans twiddle there thumbs waiting, yearning for their teams to give them that rush of adrenaline. Longing to be back on the terraces singing their hearts out for the lads.

The frustration of being stuck at home doing menial household tasks, for the sake of occupying their minds, or the boredom of going to Tesco's to do the weekly shop. Trapsing up and down isles bored out of their skulls, yearning for a fix of football. Or the tinkering about in the garden. It was over. The waiting was now over. The eternity which is the close Season had come to an end. They could come alive again. Reincarnated. They could get their fix. This is what they lived for. What meant more to them than anything else in the World. What life was all about was back where it belonged. It was back in their lives. They could be football supporters again.

'Its coming home. Its coming home. Football's coming home' could be heard reverberating around the country. Every Football League Stadium was reincarnated. The vociferous fans had discovered their vocal chords again and didn't they show it. They were squealing for their teams, the purpose of life was back with them. They were singing the football death knells of the opposition. They were singing as if their lives depended on it. They did. Everyone knows good football fans can sing their teams to victory. Everyone knows the value of a good football fan.

Saturday the 8th August was a beautiful Summer's day. Scarborough was at her best. The gardens were in full bloom. The sea was a wonderful shade of blue and the sky was cloudless. On the morning of our opening match I took a morning stroll along the seafront to relax and enjoy the beauty of the town. Scarborough's seafront is paradise on an early Summer's morning. The calm before the storm. The beach awaits her many admirers but for now she is almost alone and magnificent in her splendour.

As I sauntered along the sand I had a million scenarios of the day going through my head. Every one positive. Every one negative towards Southend United. I wondered if we could start today on a long, unbeaten run that would give us the flying start that we all so badly yearned for. There was no reason why not.

The million thoughts that filled my head were only briefly interrupted by the odd 'morning' or 'lovely day' with my other fellow early morning strollers. It was the perfect start to a beautiful day that could be made so much more beautiful with a Scarborough victory at 4.45 p.m. that afternoon.

Heading into the ground that afternoon I felt the tingle, the rush of adrenaline and the expectancy of an opening victory. The drive in was slow and steady as the flow of traffic approaching was the norm on a hot Summer, Saturday afternoon. There already was the odd splattering of spectators nearing the Stadium. They had not been evident for a few months but today they were making their way for another fix of Football League Soccer.

As I approached the Stadium I was tickled to see a great big red and white Seagull strutting up and down outside the main entrance. Our mascot Gulliver the Seagull was doing everything in his power to attract passing motorists to the fact that we were playing at the McCain Stadium that afternoon and that he was likely to 'pooh' on them if they did not attend. He blew me a great, big sickly Seagull kiss as I passed him by.

The first Saturday is unrivalled. New Season, new faces and new belief. For those who were successful, what has happened before can be maintained. For those who came close, what has happened before can be bettered. For those who had a torrid Season, what has happened before will never happen again.

We will be back

Every living, breathing football fan has had a massive injection of optimism and the moaning, pessimistic brigade are redundant. They know they will be back in force soon, but today is the day of the football optimists. Today every football fan had a giant smile on their faces.

Kick off time was upon us. We were under starters orders. The pitch looked better than it had ever done before. The groundstaff accepted the compliments bestowed upon them in the lead up to the game. They had produced a surface which cried out for football. They deserved the compliments paid. The unsung heroes. Today they could beam like Cheshire cats as they received compliment after compliment about the splendour of their pitch. A lush expanse of green, ready for football.

All the auxiliary workers who give up their time for nothing, or next to nothing, for the love of Scarborough Football Club were back where they belonged. They were back at the McCain Stadium. The Programme Sellers, the turnstile operators, the First Aid officers, the food and drink vendors, the stewards and all the others were back making their small, but significant contribution to the Club on match days.

Fans re-acquainted with fellow die-hards, they hadn't seen since the last game of the last Season. Instantly, they were the best of buddies again. Instantly, they were one. United in their love for Scarborough Football Club. They didn't talk about how things had been for themselves over the last few months. There was no time for that. They only talked about the moment. Sang for the moment. The opening game of the Season.

As usual, the Stadium wasn't exactly bursting at the rafters. Infact it was a disappointingly low attendance. A meagre 2,298 spectators, but the atmosphere was excellent. Southend had brought up a sprinkling of followers and they were doing their best to be heard. This was it. The train had arrived, the ship had come in. The aeroplane had landed. A new dawn had broken. The first whistle of the 1998/99 Season was sounded.

The game ebbed and flowed, hustled and bustled and raised the heartbeat from time to time but after 45 minutes it remained goalless and chances had been rare. But, the second half started as we had planned, the Boro' went one up. Steven Brodie, our diminutive striker, opened his goalscoring account which we all knew would be one of many. Finished with precision. The Boro' were back. We were on the march. The seagulls were back in flight. This would be the McCain fortress once again.

The McCain Stadium exploded. Or at least it popped! We were in front. The Red and White Army burst into song. Music to my ears.

Football songs are often a joy to the ear, but none moreso than the song of satisfaction. The song that is sung in recognition of their team sticking the ball in the opposition's net. 1-0, 1-0, 1-0, 1-0. We're going to win the league, we're going to win the league... How I wanted to hear such song a million times in the forthcoming weeks and months of the Season.

We had only been beaten 3 times at home in the league last Season. Our home form had been formidable. We knew this was our patch and teams would come, but we intended to send them home pointless. We had done it so often last Season. Travellers would leave empty handed. We would do it again this Season. Gifts would not be given at the McCain Stadium. League points would not be found by the opposition at Scarborough. You could try but you would fail.

One hour into the game, the impossible happened, we found ourselves level and 15 minutes later we were trailing 1-2. What had happened? The whole thing had gone pear-shaped and before we knew it we had lost our first game of the Season. We had lost at home. Our disbelieving fans departed down Seamer Road numbed by a home defeat. A defeat in our first game of the Season. The song that was in their heart earlier had now emptied as they trudged away from the Stadium.

It was a big disappointment, an anti-climax. The expectation of victory did not materialise. We were beaten and we had let our fans down. The team did not play particularly well and some of the cynics were already condemning us to the depths of the Division.

The following day the curtain-raiser for the Premier League big boys took place at Wembley with Arsenal, the Premier League Champions playing the mighty Manchester United. The 97/98 Season had been a barren one for United and they wanted to start 98/99 with the winning of the Charity Shield. Arsenal were the double winners and United's dominance had been questioned. They aimed to reclaim their crown quickly.

Under a baking hot Wembley sun United were crushed by Arsenal 3-0. With goals from Overmars, Wreh and Anelka. Arsenal produced a performance which gave a strong indication that they were ready to defend their title with conviction and looked awesome on the day. They outplayed United in every department and sent an ominous message out to all the other teams they would soon be facing in the Premier League. The Gunners looked well capable of shooting down many rivals in the Season ahead.

United, on the other hand, were a poor shadow of themselves and the long knives were already being shown by the football pundits. Had the bubble burst? Was this to be another Season without a trophy? Had Ferguson been around too long? Time would tell. One thing is always for certain, United are lead by a manager who only accepts success and have a squad of players who only know victory. The Season ahead will be a critical one for United.

When the players re-grouped on the Monday morning there was a brightness about the place. They were very quickly back down to business. Training was conducted at Bramcote. The School was devoid of children as they were on their School vacation. There was a sprinkling of inquisitive holiday makers who had ambled into the grounds to watch the team work. They must have been impressed. It was bright, quick and purposeful. The Session was concluded with the usual piece of shooting practice. When everyone gets the chance to be Alan Shearer and goalkeepers get the opportunity to pull off magnificent save after save.

Tuesday morning was not the best of mornings weather-wise. The skies had opened and it was persisting it down. It was surely not like this for the Athletico Madrid players! The morning was spent working on the shape of the team and particularly on the back four. Emphasis was placed upon holding the eighteen yard line and working strongly as a unit. The back four defended expertly and looked 'Arsenal' like during the session. The morning's work ended with defensive and attacking set plays. Mick put great emphasis on these as he regularly reminded players of the value of good set plays.

Our next game was at home on the following Wednesday to Barnsley in the Worthington Cup. We had had some fantastic nights in the past in this competition. Boro' fans relived those nights to anyone who cared to listen, a million times over. They were proud of those nights. They were there to see it with their own eyes. The brilliance of the victories had been magnified. They would become even more glorified as the years rolled by.

The nights when the mighty Chelsea were humbled at the McCain. The night when we overcame a 0-2 deficit from the first leg to give Coventry a 3-0 roasting. The night when Arsenal allegedly played at the McCain Stadium. Nobody seen them because of the pea-soup fog, but they were there and they were lucky to beat the Seadogs before going on to win the trophy. Nigel Winterburn scoring the only goal of the game and I have never forgiven him to this day. Nights never to be forgotten.

Football immortals, Shilton, Shearer and Robson had all been on previous Cup nights. Everyone wanted another glory night. Everyone wanted to see the humbling of another Premier League giant. Everyone wanted to see the silky skills of another England International. We wanted to see the Boro' complete another giant-killing act. It wasn't to be - we were beaten 0-1 and then took a 0-3 thumping at Oakwell. Our Worthington Cup run didn't get out of first gear. We were beaten convincingly without so much as causing a scare to Barnsley.

In between the Barnsley games we had travelled to Exeter and suffered another league defeat going down 0-1. The disappointment of defeat quickly paled into insignificance as news flashed throughout the country of the terrible atrocity in Omagh, Northern Ireland. Another act of mindless violence. Another loss of innocent lives. All in the cause of the so called political struggle.

On a busy Saturday afternoon on the town's High Street many innocent people perished by the bomb. Men, women and children obliterated by an I. R. A. bomb. Innocent people in the wrong place at the wrong time. The bombing received Worldwide condemnation. There had been such Worldwide condemnation many times before but still the killing and maiming went on. Would there ever be an end to such sectarian violence? Please God let the answer be yes.

In our next home game to Mansfield, before the game commenced, a minute's silence was observed for the loss of life and those injured in the carnage of Omagh. I remember praying for their deliverance into the kingdom of heaven. I remember asking for no more bloodshed and for mankind to live in harmony and share this beautiful World that we lived in. Throughout the land silence was observed.

It was another home game where we maintained our abysmal form with another 2-3 defeat in which Steven Brodie raised his goal tally to two and Gareth Williams had chipped in with the other consolation goal. This gave us the ignominy of propping up the third division. We had played three games and accumulated no points. We experienced our first taste of life at the bottom. It was not to be the last!

In the players bar after the match the conversation was as usual about the previous ninety minutes and, as usual, everyone had their opinions. Fans pay their money and they have their right to be heard. As to be expected, they were not happy with our start to the new Season. They reflected on the previous Season and how close we had gone, and gave their views of why we were languishing at the bottom of the table. Needless to say there were several different viewpoints to our current predicament.

Meanwhile the change at the top of the Club continued to mystify everyone. Everybody had expected a rapid injection of money to be made available for the acquisition of new players. They had expected a

We will be back

high-profile leader who would be seen to be a man of action, a man who would get things done. Give the Club a new direction, a thrust forward. It wasn't happening. Anton appeared to be a man of mystery and was very rarely seen or heard around the ground.

If we were mystified by some of the goings on at the McCain Stadium, what about the poor Geordies! A ball had hardly been kicked in anger when the great King Kenny was given his P45. What was the crazy reasoning in this. He had taken them to an F. A. Cup Final, been allowed to spend millions on new players, and then shown the door. Is the football world going mad?

Kenny became the first managerial casualty of the new Season. The man who had brought Premier League Championships to two previous clubs. He was the first to receive the chop, he definitely would not be the last! As the King was dethroned the football world was rife with suggestions of who would claim his crown.

There was talk that Andy Saville was about to sign for Scarborough, everything was in place for him to be our first signing under the Johnson regime. Terms had been agreed between the two Clubs. The player was happy to come. It was publicised in the local newspaper he had signed, then he hadn't, then he had and then finally the whole deal was off! What a shambles. What was going on? The fans wanted answers. They weren't forthcoming.

As we got deeper into the mess of requiring new players and money being, or not being available. Money was not appearing to be a problem at Old Trafford for Alex Ferguson. Having bought Dutch defender Jaap Stam for a meagre ten million pounds it was disclosed that Alex had raided the transfer market again. This time spending a cool twelve million on Aston Villa's Tobagan International, Dwight Yorke. This is how the other half live.

United had been searching for that striker who would unlock European defences. Many hats had been thrown into the ring. They needed another goal machine, that precious jewel that every great team needs. Was Dwight to be the solution to their problem? It was a massive fee but it costs money to buy you goals at the very top level. Would Dwight provide them with the goals that mattered? On those big European nights, in those vitally important games where two top teams horns are locked together and a master goalscorer suddenly and clinically separates them? We shall see.

Five games gone and no sign of a victory. Our next trip was to London, to the Capital, to play Leyton Orient. They had just come down and were amongst everyone's favourites to go straight back up. They had what it takes to go straight back up. We were expected to make it six defeats in a row. They were expected to get three points closer to promotion. They would play us off the park, or so they thought. Football's not always like that.

We had left Scarborough early that morning for the trip to the capital. As was the norm, the bus departed from the McCain Stadium with a distinct lack of bodies. There was only the small smidgeon of players who resided in the town, a couple of directors and the local 'scoop'. The journey down would be broken up by stops for the other players and for the customary pre-match not far from the Orient.

As usual Ray ensured everyone got on who was due to get on. Ray was regimental in his bus-conducting! Ray always has a list drawn up of who is due to get on the bus, and where they are due to embark and at what time. If the bus arrived at a service station where we are due to pick a player or players up, a few minutes early, Ray would meet the players before they climbed on board to say that they could not come on until the time shown on his schedule! As they walked past him when gaining admission he would carefully tick their names off of his travellers list. It is a standing joke between us about the precision Ray takes in undertaking this task. And provides us with a childish giggle on our travels.

We got the start we wanted. The game had barely had time to draw breath, when we found ourselves a goal up in the first minute with a goal from Liam Robinson. By Liam's own admission, goals were becoming a bit of a collector's item for him but it was another one he could notch on his goalscoring belt. It was as if Liam had scored his first ever goal. He went loopy. Further goals from Matthew Russell and Steven Brodie gave us a very impressive 3-0 away win. This was the start of a new beginning. Surely we were now ready to explode up the league? The long trip back up the M1 was a happy one. Conversation was aplenty. Spirits were high.

The month of August finished with another 1-2 defeat at home to Brighton. Fortress McCain was not living up to its reputation. Four games at home and no sign of a draw let alone a precious victory. We had taken three points from our four league games in the opening month and gone out of the Worthington Cup. It was a dismal commencement to the Season. There was not too many smiling, confident faces to be found at the McCain Stadium.

At the top end of the table Rotherham were setting the pace and newly-promoted Halifax had started very promisingly. However, as the late great

We will be back

Bill Shankly had once said, 'It's not a sprint but a Marathon' - there was a long way to go. Could these pace-setters maintain the pace or would they falter as the race developed?

Away from the football, the Summer Season was about to close its curtains. It had been a poor Season for the town of Scarborough. The inclement weather had meant fewer visitors. Fewer visitors meant less business generated and consequently many businesses, dependent on their Summer takings, suffered. It is so often said, and so very true, that if Britain could guarantee good weather, not many Brits would choose to travel abroad to spend their holidays. And no doubt, our beautiful town would be a popular destination for many.

Soon the town would belong again to the residents. Ownership returned by the holidaymakers and visitors. The town would become a little quieter and seasonal businesses would close their doors and count the cost of the lack of sunshine and the wet, Summer weather.

Like the Keep Left sign something wasn't quite right at Seamer Road! What had caused this disappointing start? The race had started but we were still in the starting blocks. Everyone had their opinion. We needed three or four players. We needed a big striker. We needed money made available. We had to get rid of certain players. We had to get rid of the Manager. The Board should go. Everyone contributed their ten penneth worth. The fact was we needed points like we needed blood, and we needed them fast. We needed a points transfusion!

The opening month had brought very little joy. Points were scarce. Our position was precarious and the natives were restless. The month of September couldn't come quick enough and the memory of August erased. It was a depressing start. Things could only get better.

6

Things can only get better

SEPTEMBER 1999

It was a very short intermission, but it was the month when competitive International football re-commenced. The qualifying stages for Euro 2000 began. England started their group matches with a visit to Sweden. Everyone knew this would be a difficult match but, after fairing so well in France, it was a match where they expected to return unbeaten.

They started on fire with Captain courageous, Alan Shearer opening his Euro account after only two minutes. England were in control until after 20 minutes the flow ceased and the game ebbed in the direction of the Swedes. In a matter of minutes after the half hour the Swedish side saw themselves 2-1 up and having the English defence on the rails.

England could not regain the rhythm they had shown in the early part of the match and to add insult to injury Paul Ince was sent off in the 67th minute. It was a poor result and a poor performance. Señor Hoddle could expect no words of comfort in the tabloids the next day. He would get the customary roasting at the hands of the Sports writers and his team would be spared no punches. It was not the start the country wanted and was not the start they needed in what would be a difficult group to qualify from, let alone win.

September saw us, unlike England, start to show a bit of form. We couldn't afford another disastrous month like August. It had to be more

We will be back

productive. We started the month with a visit to Cambridge. The land of the intellect. It was a shocking afternoon with the game in jeopardy due to torrential rain. The place was awash.

The day had started early with the team bus leaving the McCain Stadium at the crack of dawn. It was going to be a long day but hopefully a happy one. The skies were grey as we made our way out of Scarborough along the A64 and before long the rain started to come down in torrents. There was a definite possibility of a postponement as we arrived at the ground. It was a heck of a trip to make to be about-turned before having the chance to kick a ball. But, the game was played.

We started like the day. Appallingly. With two weak goals conceded in the first twenty minutes. Two defensive errors which cost us dearly. It looked like we were going to get thrashed as Cambridge continued to take the game to us and with a bit more good fortune they could have been five up before half time. But football has a habit of smacking you in the face sometimes and Cambridge got one of those smackings.

Just before half time, on one of our rare forward forays we managed to get a corner. With the referee looking at his watch and ready to draw the first half to its conclusion Jason Lydiate rose to head home in the time added on in the first half, to send us in 1-2 down. It had given us a lifeline. A glimmer of hope. We didn't deserve it but we had got it. The game should have been over but now it was a different story. Sometimes you don't want half time to come. Today we wanted it badly.

Mick was very composed considering we had under-performed. However, we were still in the game and he reasoned we could only play better in the second half, and we could still leave with maximum points. He was to be proved correct. He had seen a glaring weakness in the Cambridge backline to crosses. If we could get the ball in the box from wide angles we could get some joy.

In the second half we were a different team. We were causing the Cambridge defence major problems and ultimately we got what we were due. Two more headed goals from Alex Marinkov and Gareth Williams saw us travelling back up to Scarborough with the smile of victory on our faces. It was a brilliant win and one which we could build on. Cambridge had crumbled under our aerial threat and Mick's tactics had worked perfectly.

Those long trips back from away matches were usually passed with a game of Scrabble among the management team. It helped to pass the time and make the journey pass a little quicker. The problem was that they were fiercely competitive and a little subterfuge was not unknown. Regularly arguments would develop over the validity of certain words. Generally, if Mick said it was a word then it was a word. It didn't matter if it was not in the Oxford Dictionary. If it was one of Wadsworth's words that's all that counted.

The trip back from Cambridge followed this familiar pattern and the games followed there usual procedure. Mick usually was the victor. A Wadsworth word or two usually resulting in about fifty or sixty points and sufficient to guarantee the manager the satisfaction that not only was he a master tactician but also a master of the English language.

On disembarking from the coach and ensuring boots, kit etc. were safely stored back at the McCain Stadium Ray and I decided to wet our whistle at one of the local hostelries. It was a well earned alcoholic lubrication as we had served the Club well throughout the day and witnessed the team take an excellent three points from a strong Cambridge side.

On the Monday it was diagnosed that Kevin Martin our young 'keeper had ruptured his cruciate ligament. This was a devastating blow to everyone, especially Kevin. The poor boy had only recently returned from a lengthy injury due to the rupturing of cruciate ligaments in his other leg. He had fought so determinedly to come back and then for him to receive this setback. Clearly, very hard for him to take.

Kevin was informed of his injury by Mick and it all was too much for him to take. He broke down at the news he was going to be out of football again for a long period of time. He had done so well to recover so quickly from his last operation and now this freak injury had happened.

Kevin is a great lad. A Midlands boy. A strong, resilient and proud young man and he will be back. Of that you can be sure. This was a major setback to his career but he had overcome his last cruciate ligament rupture. He would do it again.

Football, to many, is a game of glamour and glory and not too many people realise the down-side of the game. The disappointment of being dropped. The frustration of being injured. The uncertainty of being released. The tragedy of having to give the game up prematurely. Football is a very precarious occupation, fiercely competitive and full of abject disappointments as well as the highs. For every feel-good story there are one hundred sad songs to be sung.

Shrewsbury were the next visitors to the McCain Stadium. It was Wednesday the 9th. Again the crowd was below 2,000. This was disappointing to everyone. The town was crying out for the Club to buy new

We will be back

players but if they didn't show on match days, we couldn't provide the money to invest in the players they so much said we needed. Money just could not be conjured out of thin air.

We followed up our victory at Cambridge with our first home points. They were a long time coming but very welcomed when they arrived. Liam Robinson and Steven Brodie had given us the goals which had given us the first win on our own patch. Shrewsbury were the team at the bottom of the table on this date, and, to be fair it showed. They didn't cause us any real problems and they looked like a side that, if they did not turn things round quickly, they would very soon find themselves in deep soup.

This was more like the Scarborough we all expected. Six points from the last two games. Maximum gain. Surely we were now heading in the right direction and we could start to make our way to the top of the tree and start to look like a team capable of winning the Championship. Six points taken off two teams who will definitely be there or thereabouts for promotion in May.

During this month the Latin temperament of Sheffield Wednesday's brilliant Italian Paulo Di Canio went off the Richter scale when Paulo lost his marbles during a fierce game with the Premier Champions, Arsenal. His reaction to a decision by referee Paul Alcock which resulted in his dismissal was sufficient to deny Paulo the opportunity of displaying his blinding talent for nine matches. It brought universal disapproval from everyone within the game and was an act that surely could not be seen again!

The take-over of the Club was strange to say the least. Everything was not as it should be. There was still uncertainty and doubt in who actually owned the Club and why was it taking so long to administer the transition? Clearly, this was causing frustration to the management team and the players. They wanted it resolving and knowing exactly what was the way forward for the Club. This was a period in the Club's history which would have a detrimental effect the likes of which had never been witnessed before.

In this month the Club was informed that two of its young players had been chosen to represent England at Under 15 level. This was a magnificent boost for everyone involved with the Youth Policy and a fantastic achievement for the two boys. For a little, unfashionable Club like Scarborough to have two players selected for England was unbelievable. The Club had put in place a Youth Policy which was starting to pay dividends and this would be seen as the Season progressed.

We will be back

Our next game was a journey to Wales and our first defeat in the month. We went 0-2 down to Swansea before returning to winning ways with an emphatic 3-1 win at home to Brentford, on the following Saturday.

This was one of our best wins of the Season and one of the best performances. We were outstanding against a very impressive Brentford and thoroughly deserved our result. This was to take us to our highest league position in the league as the Season unfolded. We thought it was the springboard to success. It also saw Neil Radigan make his first team debut. Neil was another young player who had come through the Youth system.

September saw the commencement of the Champions League. Would this be the year when English football could be restored to being the Masters of Europe? Our two representatives, Arsenal, the English Premier League Champions and Manchester United the Premier League runners-up. The first time the Competition had been opened up to non-championship winning teams from various European countries.

United started their campaign with a massive game at Old Trafford against the Spanish giants Barcelona and Arsenal went to France to face the French side Lens. Both teams taking one point in what could so easily have been three. United letting slip a 2-0 half time lead to draw 3-3 and Arsenal conceding a goal with almost the last kick of the game to draw 1-1.

Arsenal followed up this result on the last day of the month with a magnificent 2-1 win over the Greek champions Panathinaikos at Wembley with two goals from their superb Centre Backs Adams and Keown. This was a brilliant start for Arsenal but United dropped another valuable two points in Germany when they conceded an equalising goal by Bayern Munich in the 90th minute to leave the score finishing at 2-2. United had taken only two points from the first six on offer. Would this mean them faltering at the first stage?

Our last game in September saw us travel to Plymouth where we fought out, literally fought out a 0-0 draw. We finished the game with nine men. Our old warrior John Kay taking a premature bath due to a second cautionable offence and Paddy Atkinson having to be carried off after a fierce tackle from behind.

It was a superb away point under the circumstances. We had now established a position of respectability in the league. We had taken ten points from fifteen in the month and this was the sort of form we all expected to happen way back in May and this was the sort of form we

We will be back

would need to consistently achieve if we were going to get the promotion we so badly wanted.

Again we had used one of our youngsters who had developed through our Youth system. This time big Michael McNaughton made his debut. Michael was affectionately named 'The Beast' by those around the Club, and Michael came through his baptism with flying colours. He performed heroically on the night. Michael was 'The Beast' by name but certainly not by nature.

The journey had been long. I'm sure Marco Polo didn't have to travel as far as this on his epic journey. We did not get back into Scarborough until the wee, wee hours of Thursday morning. We returned 'Zombie' like, totally bus-lagged. This is a condition ten times worse than jet-lagged and similar to the walking dead. Finally, arriving in the sanctuary of our own home and the luxury of our own beds just as the day was breaking.

The nights were starting to become darker, quicker as Winter showed her cold face again and the nights ahead for Scarborough Football Club would grow darker and colder as the Season progressed.

Thursday was a day of rest and recovery for everyone. Training would resume on Friday morning. However, the coaching staff were in. A little later than normal it must be said, but they were in. We discussed the previous nights efforts and talked about the many positives from the night and the situation with regard to injuries and suspension. The meeting was concluded with Mick inviting us to lunch at the Olivers Mount Cafe. A cafe beautifully situated overlooking the picturesque bay on Scarborough's South side.

Towards the end of the month the Club received a strong letter condemning the behaviour of Gulliver. Gulliver, as you know, was a Seagull. He was our mascot and he had been a silly Seagull. Prior to our match with the Bees, the bird had not just been flapping its wings, it had been wiggling its bum. In the direction of the disgusted, and deeply offended Brentford fans. My word what a disgraceful act to do. Surely this would bring the game into disrepute!

Fortunately Gulliver didn't have the capability to unload any waste from his posterior but his actions were enough to cause anger among the away supporters. I ask you, what's the World coming to! There's people being wiped out in Kosovo and these people are getting upset about a stupid Seagull wiggling its botty. Turn the other cheek!

Now, I must tell you, I have a thing about Football Club mascots. Billy the Bull, Charlie the Cheeky Monkey and Peter the Pillock. I have to say they are not one of my loves in the game of football. In fact, I find them a complete pain in the posterior. What is their point? Do they need to exist? Do they really add to the attraction of a football match? I think not. Some of them are actually starting to gain superstar status with their ridiculous antics but I would still rather see them at such places as childrens' parties and Disneyland. Not strutting their stuff at football grounds up and down the country.

On the final Saturday in September Scarborough's favourite son, The Yorkshire Hunter, Paul Ingle stopped Billy Hardy in the 8th to become the Champion of Europe. This was a fabulous feat by Paul and one which was richly deserved. Paul had brought great credit to himself and his hometown of Scarborough. Everyone was so proud of his magnificent achievement. There was now talk of a fight with Prince Naseem. The talk was later to become fact. Bring on the Prince.

7

Who does own Scarborough Football Club?

OCTOBER 1998

As October began, Autumn took hold, and, as the leaves despatched themselves from the trees, we despatched ourselves from the foot of the table taking 13 points from our ten Football League games. We would not see another rich month such as September for a long time.

The month of October would offer another six games and a total of 18 points to play for. Mick had come close to being named manager of the month in September and we all hoped for the same type of harvest to be reaped from the points on offer in October. We started the month in a position of respectability. We would finish the month in a position of discomfort.

At every professional football Club there is a daily delivery of mail enquiring about trials and trialists. Regularly incoming telephone calls are from people requesting the opportunity to show their skills, and informing us of their belief they were the best football players since the invention of the wheel.

We frequently get letters from someone saying they have discovered the next Pele or that they have seen another David Beckham playing against their Sunday League team. Like all Clubs we have to listen. We cannot turn a blind eye and later find that a letter we received and didn't action contained a name which has come back to haunt us.

I have to say, particularly at Schoolboy level some clubs are almost paranoid about missing a boy. They have trials almost every day of the week, looking at a million young players and going frantic if they find out the boy has been asked to go to another Club later on. My philosophy is you will miss someone. It is inevitable. But, work with the boys you have got and let's see if you have got the developmental skills to produce good young footballers.

This is a policy which is readily endorsed by the management team at the Club. We understand the very best of the naturally talented boys will find themselves heading towards the bigger, richer clubs than ours and consequently we have to ensure the developmental work we do with the young players must be, not just as good, as those clubs, but better. I often say to the Youth Development Staff that we may not get the best young footballers coming to our Club but we can get the best from the young players we have at the Club.

The Programme of work we have put together at Scarborough Football Club in the development of our Schoolboys is one which we feel will enable us to get the best from the boys registered with us and provide us with technically sound, tactically aware young players when they start at the club full time on the Soccer Scholarship scheme.

In this month we invited a particular young man to come and train with us for a few days. We had a telephone call from some very enthusiastic scout informing us he had just seen the next Michael Owen. 'Michael the Second' arrived on the Monday ready to show us his phenomenal talent!

Now, sometimes you don't need to be the best observer of young talent to know whether someone has the makings of a player. Sometimes it can smack you in the eye within minutes that he has got what it takes, and sometimes you don't even need to see him play, to know that he will never be a footballer as long as he has a whole in his bottom! This was one of those cases.

'Michael the Second' was seen outside putting out his last cigarette before training. He got changed ready to impress. He certainly was an eye-catcher. He had fluorescent yellow boots, a British Bull dog tattooed on his thigh, about fourteen ear rings in each ear and brilliant red hair! A cross between Russ Abbott and Johnny Rotten.

Within fifteen minutes of training, in fact I don't think we had completed our warm-up 'Michael was breathing out of his proverbial! As training progressed I'm afraid Michael did not. He went from bad to worse. Although he was due to spend a few days with us, 'Michael' did a Lord

We will be back

Lucan and was never seen again. I don't think he will be one who comes back to haunt us, unless he asks for another trial!

On the 3rd October Chester City made the long trip across the Pennines to the McCain Stadium. On their last visit we emphatically beat them 4-1 and were very worthy of the scoreline. It was not to be a repetition of the fixture from the year before. We did not play well and were tortured by Rod Thomas, one of Mick's ex-players from his Carlisle days. Rod tore us inside out as we were humbled 2-4.

Mick had been saying this was the calibre of player he needed to strengthen his squad and to give us the cutting edge we required if we were to make a serious assault on the third division title. That afternoon his view was endorsed by the Boro' faithful. They knew we needed the addition of a little finesse and Rod Thomas could give us that piece of magic they wanted to see. The flair player with the finesse to unlock defences. Rod Thomas, nor any player of his ilk would display their talent in a Boro shirt before the end of the Season.

Before our next game, their was some scouting to be done. We had to run the eye over a couple of players who we thought might just be players who could do a job for us, albeit on loan. On the Tuesday and Wednesday night we took in several games. Our spying missions proved fruitless. The players we went particularly to watch did not set our heartbeats racing and there would be no new additions for our next outing.

We then travelled to Carlisle to play the team where Mick had achieved his greatest managerial success. It was a match played on a Friday night. We travelled up through the day and came back late in the evening empty-handed. This was a game that Mick, and most managers returning to their former clubs, was eager to win. To put one over on their former employers. We fought like tigers but got suckered late in the second half by a soft goal. We deserved something but got something which would appear all to familiar as the Winter months rolled by. Nothing.

Mick is a living legend in Carlisle. In his spell of managing the Cumbrian side he had given them the third division championship and taken them to Wembley in the same Season. He had brought back a lot of respectability to the Club after it had spent some time in the doldrums. He was welcomed back but their welcome did not extend to a three point welcome.

Down in London, George Graham was doing the unimaginable. The former Arsenal manager was taking over as manager of the enemy, Tottenham Hotspur. Did he have no scruples? This was almost sacreligious how could the Tottenham fans possibly accept a Gunner? How could 'boring, boring Arsenal fans' ever forgive him?

Leeds United didn't want him to leave, the work he had completed in his short time at Elland Road was admired by everyone, especially by those within the Club and they were desperate for him to see the job through. There plea for him to stay would be in vain.

George, it was said, was missing living in London. He wanted to return. He fancied the challenge of taking Tottenham back to where they had belonged and, in October, he became the new manager at White Hart Lane. Could he be accepted by the Tottenham faithful? Would he ever be forgiven by the Arsenal fans? Leeds fans branded him a Judas.

Our next game was a home match against our local rivals Hull City. If our Season had started badly, Hull's had started worse! They were rock-bottom. The Club was in turmoil and the fans were baying for blood. How could a club of such stature be propping up the Football League? They were too big a Club to be bottom, but they were. They had only picked up one point from their previous five excursions and discontent was rife among their Humberside following. The execution squad were waiting to execute.

We were meeting Hull at the right time. They were wrapped up in a web of uncertainty. There was no money to be had. They wanted their manager Mark Hateley out, but couldn't afford to sack him. The fans were seething with the Club's owner David Lloyd and they were in a terrible run. They were surely there for the taking. If there was a time to face anyone, this was it. They were a club with problems.

The take over of our Club was becoming a standing joke. We were now into the middle of October and nobody knew who was the rightful owner of the Club. Was it Anton Johnson? Was it John Russell? It might as well have been Billy the Fish. What the hell was going on? The fans demanded answers and a quick solution. If it was Anton Johnson, stand up and say so. If it wasn't he must clear off and not come back.

The uncertainty persisted. A fans forum was arranged for Friday the 30th October in the McCain Lounge. Everything would become a little clearer. It didn't. That particular week saw a rainfall which was the Mother of all rainfalls and the roof of the McCain Lounge succumbed to the weight of the precipitation, and came tumbling in. Meeting cancelled. Spectators seething! Was this an Act of God or an Act of Anton?

The Scarborough Evening News disclosed the result of its recent competition. The fans had the opportunity to write in to the paper and name their all time favourite Boro' player. The winner was Jeff Barmby, father of Nick Barmby the Everton and England player. Jeff had been at the Club during the height of its non-league days. He was greatly revered by followers of this time and many a fan from those days loved to tell the tale of the brilliance of Barmby. How we could have done with a man of Jeff's ability at this time. None of our current squad of players featured in the all-time great list!

During the latter end of the month our young striker Chris Tate was added to the list of long-term injuries. Chris had a stress fracture in his foot which would keep him sidelined for at least six weeks. Chris was to become an outstanding success as the Season matured, and who knows, if this injury had not occurred, maybe Chris would have been the answer to our offensive play, sooner.

As was to be expected. we had our biggest home league gate of the Season against the Tigers. And, as to be expected, when we have a bigger audience we under-perform. When we are expected to produce the goods we deliver nothing. We went down 1-2 with a goal from Jamie Hoyland unable to stave off the stigma of losing to our arch-rivals and defeat giving Hull their first three points from an away fixture. This bridged the gap between the sides not just by points but by places as well, taking us within touching distance of Hull and giving us the unenviable position of being second to bottom in the third division of the Nationwide League. There were rumblings. It was not a happy sanctuary and unity was expectedly in question.

In this month Manchester United gave notice to the rest of Europe that this was a team capable of winning the Champions league by going to Brondby and beating the Danes by 6-2. To score six away from home against a side who had in the previous month beaten Bayern Munich sent shock waves through European Club football. United were absolutely awesome on the night and gave out the message they were now ready to be crowned Champions of Europe.

On the same evening Arsenal again conceded a goal in the last minute of the game against Dynamo Kiev at the National Stadium. They had accumulated five creditable points from their first three games in Europe, but it could so easily have been nine.

Their next game would be away to Kiev in Russia and they knew they would be without their flying Dutchman, Denis Bergkamp, or should I say non-flying Dutchman as Denis has a fear of flying. A very crucial game in the history of Arsenal Football Club and one which they would have to play without their most influential player. There was no way they could consider getting him there by land.

As the might of Arsenal and Manchester United carried the flag in Europe for British Clubs we were carrying the weight of almost every club in the Football League on our shoulders. We were down in the dungeons of despair looking up enviably at other sides in positions of respectability and promise.

We had to find the match to ignite our Season. A slice of consistency to provide us with a run of results to escalate us up the division. We had displayed the odd good performance, but not nearly regularly enough, and too often, had given displays of football which did not deserve to win games.

We then travelled to Barnet midweek to get a well-earned 0-0 draw and finished the month with a 1-1 draw at home to Torquay. Our home game against Rochdale had fallen victim to the weather but we would be playing them next month at home in our F. A. Cup first round tie.

So, October finished with us taking a meagre two points from 15. This was a terrible return and the natives were getting restless. September, which had been so fruitful, was now a distant memory. What was happening? How could a team which had come so close just a few months ago look like a side so far away. We were languishing in the basement of the table and did not look like we were able to force the wind of change.

Chris Tait, Scarborough's prolific young goalscorer

8

Russell's return

NOVEMBER 1998

We were now going into the fourth month of the Season. It was, to say the least, not going as we expected. We had had a disastrous August, a decent September and a woeful October. Talk about a roller-coaster of a Season. We needed to have a successful November. We had to get into the groove and start producing the goods.

Seven games were to be played in the month of November. Five in the league and two in the F. A. Cup. Our record in the F. A. Cup since joining the league was disappointing. If ever there was a Season to lay that ghost to rest it was this Season. We desperately needed a Cup run to ignite the Season and to bring some much-needed coffers into the Club. We had been drawn against Rochdale at home. Not the most glamorous of ties but, after all, it was a home draw, so we had to be pleased. A visit to Old Trafford would come later. If only!

Before we set off on the long road to Wembley and F. A. Cup glory we had two difficult away trips to Rotherham and Cardiff. We needed points. We wanted to go into the Cup on the back of some confidence-building results with some valuable points in the bag but we went into the Cup with the memory of two recent defeats, no points and confidence about as prominent as a baboon doing the La Bamba in Bradford! We hadn't won in our last eight games and we were fully aware of our plight.

We will be back

The long road to Wembley turned into a short step to dismay. We had a lacklustre draw at home to Rochdale before saying farewell to another year of what might have been as we were beaten 0-2 at Spotland. We were out and to make matters worse, Hull City had got through and would play the Premiership leaders Aston Villa at Villa Park! Talk about rubbing salt into the wound. The Chairman would have killed for a money-spinning fixture like this.

In between our two meetings in the Cup with Rochdale was sandwiched an away fixture between the two Clubs. Matthew Russell, the Chairman's eldest son brought the vital goal which gave us our first league win in nine and which gave us three points which we needed like fish need water. It was a bitterly cold night in Rochdale with temperatures near freezing point. The attendance was not exactly capacity and when we scored the only noise to be heard was from half a dozen hardened Seasiders who had made the trip across the Pennines.

Travelling supporters to watch the Boro' were becoming fewer in number. Never mind travelling supporters, our home support was suffering the same significance. Many people who stopped you in the street or in the supermarket would express their discontent at the ineptness of the team's performances. Many stating they would not waste their hard-earned money on a miserable Saturday afternoon's entertainment at the McCain Stadium. We needed to start providing performances to attract the disillusioned back through the gates.

Our next two fixtures were against our north-east neighbours Hartlepool and Darlington. Never easy fixtures and often volatile. After a 1-2 defeat at home to Hartlepool we went up to Darlington expecting a change of fortune. Needing that change of fortune. But again, not getting it.

It was to be the first league appearance of our recent Scandinavian signing, Thomas Dablesteen, and big things were expected of the man from Denmark. Mick seen him as being a player who could give us the sparkle we had been missing. The sparkle at Darlington lasted as long as the sparkle from a cheap bottle of Champagne. Thomas's performance was ineffective and the team were booed off the park on the face of a 0-3 defeat, on a pitch which had to be said resembled a newly-ploughed farmer's field.

Darlington had apparently spent a fortune at the beginning of the Season on their pitch. They are a side who try to play football so they obviously wanted a pitch where football could be played. Unfortunately they now had a pitch more suitable for mud wrestling. It was in terrible

We will be back

condition and they had a pitch which they clearly were very unhappy with. And rightly so.

In contrast, they had recently developed Feethams and had a Stand that they can be very proud of. An excellent seated area with a labyrinth of rooms ideal for functions and providing excellent office space for administrational duties. It is a Stand that must be the envy of many lower league sides who generally find themselves very short of required space and have inappropriate room for functions and conferences and other finance-generating events.

The Quakers had quite a connection with our Club as their player-coach was the big footballing Rolls Royce, Gary Bennett, who had done such a fantastic job for us in our play-off Season and John Murray, Mr. Punch, our previous physio was now healing the sick at Darlington. Also, Gary Himsworth now plying his trade here was an ex-player of ours. So it was very nice to renew old acquaintances with them.

To make matters worse at Darlington, our number one goalkeeper Tony Elliot damaged his back. It was the recurrence of an old injury. An injury which had previously kept Tony out of football for a lengthy period when he was at Cardiff City. This time it would force Tony into early retirement! We didn't know it at the time but Darlington was to be Tony's final game for Scarborough in the Football League. A tragic day for Tony and a big loss to Scarborough Football Club.

He would later be forced into retirement and have his footballing career prematurely ended. Tony was in his prime and it was a cruel end for him in his footballing career. Not only a very good goalkeeper but one of life's true gentlemen.

As our other 'keeper Kevin Martin was rehabilitating from his cruciate ligament operation we only had one 'keeper left on the books. That was Philip Naisbett, a non-contract goalkeeper who had recently been released by Sunderland, but even Philip was carrying an injury!

We hurriedly enquired about other 'keepers and eventually took on loan Luke Weaver from Sunderland, a young 'keeper with big potential, but very little games experience. Luke would play six games for us before returning to Sunderland. Young Philip Naisbett would play two games and another young goalkeeper from Nottingham Forest, Mark Goodlad, would play three games for us. Those young 'keepers played through December, January and February for us. With all due respect to those young boys they were not the answer to our problem at this time. Given time, they will be excellent 'keepers but our situation was not the situation for a young goalkeeper to learn his trade. The significance of goalkeepers to our Season was to become incredible as the Season unfolded.

It was in this month that John Russell took his first steps to regaining control of the Club. The indecision had gone on too long. John was clearly upset by the mess the Club was in. He stated in the Papers that the Club could not purchase any new players as there was an outstanding amount of money owed to the Professional Footballers Association who had assisted in paying the players' wages recently. The Club needed to find money to clear this debt. Under the ruling, if a Club borrows money from the Professional Footballers Association, they cannot purchase new players until the debt is repaid.

Gareth Williams one of Mick's first signings was put on the transfer list at his own request. Gareth lived in Derby and was finding it increasingly difficult to make the long journeys from home to Scarborough. Before the end of the month Gareth had moved on to Hull City for a fee of £25,000. This did not go down too well with the Boro' fans. What were we doing selling one of our better players to our relegation rivals, Hull City! Sometimes money dictates. Gareth wanted away. We desperately needed an influx of cash and Hull City were prepared to buy. So it was with a bit of regret we bid farewell to 'Gripper'.

Whilst November was another barren month for us it was another excellent month for the Red Devils in Europe but a disastrous one for Arsenal. Manchester followed up their 6-2 away win at Brondby with a 5-0 home win over the Danish side. Again producing football of the highest calibre. They then took an away point at Barcelona with a fantastic 3-3 draw in the Neau Camp Stadium. This was a game that had everyone enthralled. It had everything. Brilliant football, brilliant goals. A brilliant match to remember.

It wasn't the same for Arsenal. After such a promising start they faltered big-time with a 1-3 defeat in Kiev, in weather more suitable for Yaks than footballers and then going down at home to Lens. This left Arsenal rooted to the bottom of Group E with five points. Both Dynamo Kiev and Lens had eight points but both teams had taken four points off of Arsenal in the two games they had played them. This meant there was no way back for the Gunners. Their last game against Panathinaikos in Greece was irrelevant. Regardless of the score they would not progress to the next stage. The month of November brought Arsenal in Europe roughly the same as the month of November brought

We will be back

the Seadogs in the Nationwide Third Division.

Certain things were becoming evident at the Club which had to be kept behind closed doors. Things were not harmonious. There was great disillusionment in certain quarters and the togetherness that was necessary and so vital in the face of adversity was not to be found. We had taken too few points from the points which were there to be won and discontent was setting in. We were coming to the tail end of the year and were firmly at the tail end of the table.

Although it was a far from perfect situation we found ourselves in, there was no need for panic. After all there was more than half of the Season left. There was time to correct the damage. It needed composure, clarity and direction. If we were to make progress it required unity, trust and honesty. Times were tough. But, when times are tough, the tough get going. Were we tough enough?

9

No festive cheer

DECEMBER 1998

December and football in Scarborough don't usually go together. Anyone who might be tempted to come and see the beautiful game played at the McCain Stadium most definitely wouldn't be persuaded to do so on a cold, December afternoon. There had to be far better things to do. Like sit in front of a nice fire. In a Shackleton's high chair, with a glass of claret in one's hand, reminiscing about earlier life in another part of the country, prior to retirement years in the Winter bleak of Scarborough. There are not many football crazy octogenarians to be found in our coastal town and big gates at the McCain Stadium are about as rare as a fish wearing water wings! Especially in December.

The month started with a deluge of snow. Not just a covering, it snowed like there was no tomorrow! It was the Mother of all Snowfalls! Training was scheduled for ten o'clock Monday morning. Forget it. There was no chance of it happening. Scarborough was one of the places most affected. Inland had escaped its wrath. Scarborough resembled the Arctic Circle.

Players travelling in from a distance had to be informed not to come. Not many of our players actually resided in Scarborough. Many travelled in from the North East, others journeyed from across the Pennines. Some made their way from South Yorkshire. It would have been a complete waste of time and would have been too risky for them to drive on

We will be back

the extremely hazardous roads into the town. Ski maybe. Drive, no!

Training was greatly affected for several days. The only training we could do was done indoors. We were fortunate that local schools and the town's sports centre would allow us access to their sports halls, at the expense of other members of the public. The players didn't complain too loudly as they loved nothing better than a game of head tennis or five-a-sides. And they especially didn't complain when outside was like a great big fridge-freezer.

Eventually, after what seemed an age of relative inactivity, we arranged an outside training session in Tadcaster. Tadcaster is about forty five miles from Scarborough, but at least there we would be provided a surface where work could be carried out. It was great to see grass again. Everyone had been moving around Scarborough like Torvill and Dean for the last umpteen days and now we could revert to our natural surroundings!

Our first game in the month was not until the 12th, due to the first Saturday being given to those lucky sods who had progressed into the second round of the F. A. Cup. We had fallen at the first hurdle and had to wait patiently and enviously on those sides who still had the opportunity to achieve some fame.

We were at home to the new kids on the block, Halifax Town who had recently returned to the Football League from the Nationwide Conference. They were riding on the crest of a wave. They had got off to a flyer and were creating a bit of a stir since their re-entry. Just like several other newcomers to the league they had started like a house on fire and proving the jump from the Conference League to the Football League was certainly not too big.

We had been in the same position as Halifax in Season 1987/88 when we were the first side to gain automatic promotion from the Conference into the Football League, and, like Halifax, we started our first campaign in the Football League with a flurry, sitting on top of the League at one stage and throughout that Season remaining in the top half of the Division.

In their final games in their respective groups, Manchester United fought out a 1-1 draw at Old Trafford against Bayern Munich and Arsenal had a great 3-1 victory in Greece. It was too late for Arsenal they were eliminated from the Competition but Manchester United progressed to the knock out stages, finishing as runners-up in their group behind Bayern. If United could go on and achieve European glory they were certainly doing it the hard way. They had entered the Competition as Runners-Up in their league. They were now progressing to the knock out stage of the competition as Runners-Up in their Group.

We will be back

United would now meet the mighty Inter Milan in the quarter finals. Not particularly a team of unknowns with the likes of Ronaldo, Baggio, Zamorano and Djorkeaff in the side! It would be a mouth-watering tie and a huge test of how far the mighty Reds had come. United could now put Europe to bed for a few months and concentrate on the domestic front. This put the fear of God up English football.

The Chairmanship of the Club was now back in the hands of John Russell. Anton Johnson had acrimoniously bade farewell to the Club and it has to be said many people thought it was not a day too soon. He had not brought to the Club the promises he had made and in some peoples' eyes had left the Club in a state which would be very difficult to recover from. John Russell put an impassioned plea to the supporters of the Club and to people in the town that they were needed if they were to assist the Club in maintaining its football league status. It was a message written in vain! There was absolutely no response.

Mick had spoken through the week to the coaching staff about the high-flying Halifax and the threat they posed. We knew much of their play came through the passing of their little midfielder Jamie Paterson. It was decided that we would counter this threat by man-marking Paterson and Jason Lydiate was given the job of stifling Paterson's midfield ingenuity. It worked a treat. Jason stuck to Paterson like glue and carried out his man-marking duties magnificently. Halifax never got into any rhythm. They couldn't get their game going. Paterson was ineffective and a Steven Brodie goal gave us the victory we yearned. It was a tactical success and very satisfying for the Coaching staff and the players.

On the last game before Christmas we found no festive cheer from a visit to Peterborough, going down 1-3. Thomas Dablesteen being the scorer of our single goal. His first for the Club, and his last. Thomas was close to kicking his last ball for the Club and I don't think he will be a future recipient of a testimonial at Scarborough! He would figure in just five uneventful matches and would soon be winging his way back to Denmark. He left with mixed reviews. To some he had good skill. To others he didn't have the required attributes of a footballer fighting in the fury of the third division.

In this month, in the Season of goodwill to all men, the allied forces unleashed an air raid on Iraq. Operation Desert Fox. That sly old fox Saddam had been up to his old tricks again. The old monkey had devilishly been building up another arsenal of devastation. He thought us silly-billys from the West wouldn't detect his misbehaviour. The British

We will be back

and Americans took action after being denied access to inspection of certain military sites in Iraq. Again, a drastic situation was developing in the Middle East. Why can't poor old Saddam give us some respite. Can't he retire to the Coast like other senior citizens and leave the World to be a better place!

We had two more games to play before we moved into 1999 but before them we had Christmas Day. Initially, the players were informed they would have to train as normal but Mick's festive spirit took over and he allowed them the day at home with their families. They were expected not just to eat, drink and be merry, but to do a gentle run and a few stretches at some time during the day. Hopefully, the gentle run wouldn't just be to the toilet and the few stretches up to get another can of lager from the fridge! We knew it wouldn't!

The remaining two games of the year did not bring any more festive fun. Christmas was as kind to Boro' as Saddam Hussein is to American charities. Boro' fans would not receive any football, festive cheer. On Boxing Day they made the journey down the M1 to Mansfield. It was not a day for sunglasses and flip flops. It was batten down the hatches and hold on to your hats. There was a force fifteen gale blowing and the art of standing upright could not be mastered in these hurricane conditions, let alone try to pass a football!

We found ourselves trailing 0-3 and in danger of being blown off the face of the Earth. The conditions were diabolical but the team stuck to its task and rallied with two late goals through the gentle giant Michael McNaughton and Chris Greenacre, our affable loan-signing from Manchester City. We fought for a share of the spoils but it was not to be.

This game saw young Shaun Rennison make his first team debut, another boy coming from the Club's youth policy. Shaun was to make a big impact in the first team with some very mature performances in the months ahead. I'm sure his debut he will always remember. If not for the thrill of playing for the first team for the first time then for the fact that he had survived, and lived through a Hurricane!

In our final game of the year we were humiliated by a very impressive Scunthorpe side. It was not to be our last humiliation handed out by Scunthorpe. We were outclassed in every department and were very fortunate to escape with just a 1-4 mauling. They played with purpose, with adventure and with craft and were very much worth their three points taken. We were again on the receiving end of our supporters' wrath. They were despondent and many departed from the ground long

We will be back

before the salvation of the sound of the referee's whistle. In fact you could get more people into a Mini Cooper than there was in the Stadium when the game was concluded. Three points from twelve in December.

Eight points from the last forty two. Second bottom of the table and the gap above appearing to be widening. It was a depressing situation. It was a dire situation but another year was about to arrive. Another year had to bring better results. Things had to get better. Things would get better. After all there was another sixty six points up for grabs. Was there any need for concern?

In the final days of the year our young, talented striker, Neil Campbell was close to signing for second division Colchester United. But at the last moment all parties couldn't agree and the deal was ditched. Neil did not have long to wait before he was plying his trade elsewhere. He wanted to get away. He was not happy at the Club and he needed a change to regain his confidence and belief in himself.

Interestingly, as we said goodbye to 1998 three of the top four teams in the Nationwide Third Division would remain in automatic promotion places. Cardiff, Brentford and Cambridge were all vying for the top spot and this is the way it would remain right up to the final day of the Season.

The New Year Bells of 1999 were about to ring. A few drinks would be swallowed and a few dances would be danced. Resolutions would be made by many and many people would be looking for better times ahead. Scarborough Football Club were looking for better times in the year ahead. It was onwards and upwards for us.

10

Wadsworth waves goodbye!

JANUARY 1999

With the introduction of a New Year came the announcement of the Queen's Honour List and much to my disgust there was no inclusion of my name. The World of football was recognised with Trevor Brooking receiving the C. B. E. and Stuart 'Count on me to put you out of the World Cup' Pearce being awarded the M. B. E. But nothing for Ian Kerr! I had been secretly hoping for a wee Knighthood. I had provisionally booked my top hat and tails in readiness for my trip to Buckingham Palace. My services to football and humanity in general remained unrecognised by Lizzie the Second!

With Christmas and New Year now behind the general public, normality could be restored. That lovely period in the year when works close down, holidays are given and the working person can just eat, drink and be merry. Football at the Professional rank is one of those occupations where we are excluded from such luxuries. Life must go on. There is no extended break for the footballer. There can be no over-indulgence and, if anything, work is increased.

So when anyone cares to mention that the life of a footballer is a doddle tell them from me to go and take a running jump. From July to May days off are few and far between. Its only during the month of June can you safely assume you will get a decent break to recharge your batteries. But, I wouldn't change it for the World!

We will be back

The first Saturday of the New Year saw the introduction of the Premier League giants into the F. A. Cup. It was the third round and the start of the real action in the Cup. The third round provided its usual quota of shocks with West Ham, Nottingham Forest and Aston Villa all exiting at the expense of lower league opposition. Coventry were the biggest victors of the day with a shattering 7-0 victory over Sammy McIlroy's Macclesfield.

The third round of the F. A. Cup hadn't disappointed. The most exciting competition in the globe had lived up to its reputation. Again, the mighty had fallen and the minnow had risen. Never a year goes by without the Cup throwing up a major shock or a massive slice of football theatre. This year was no exception.

Our first game of the New Year was lost to the elements. Typical of our Club's luck. A potentially finance-generating match, on a Bank Holiday, got postponed due to circumstances beyond the control of the Club. We needed this game badly. We didn't get it. Had somebody at the Club done something to upset that great man in the sky? I would ask myself that question again many times over in the month of May. The pitch was totally waterlogged and fishing would have been more appropriate than football at the McCain Stadium. It resembled the Hudson River.

It goes without saying that the smaller clubs have to scrimp and scrape to survive. We are no exception. Money has to be found and players' wages have to be paid. It is never easy to balance the books and it is a never-ending battle to keep the wolves from the door. Bank Holiday matches are games which every small Club depends upon and when they are denied it throws a great big spanner in the works. Nothing seemed to be going in our favour. Already the New Year had brought some of the old years' misfortunes.

To compound the difficult financial times, the Club was broken into and expensive video equipment was stolen. Equipment necessary for the Crowd Safety officers on match days. Without which matches would not be sanctioned by the Safety Authorities. Incidental to the financial implications of such mindless theft was the disappointment of the damage caused. We could ill-afford this regular disregard for the Club. We would have to remedy the loss of the equipment and re-secure the locks and doors which had been forced open.

Early in the New Year there was better news elsewhere. Prince Edward and Sophie announced that they were soon to be man and wife. The Queen's youngest son was to become a married man. The date of the wedding was yet to be set but already the tabloids were speculating dates and whereabouts. Would this be the start of every part of poor Sophie's life, like Diana's before, being dissected and put under the microscope of the gutter press? Everyone at Scarborough Football Club wished them well, but as far as I know they did not reciprocate and send a good luck message to us in our time of trouble!

The premiere of the highly acclaimed film 'Little Voices' was held in Scarborough at the Stephen Joseph Theatre in the Round. The film was shot on location in Scarborough and starred among others Michael Caine and Ewan McGregor. It opened to rave reviews and was an instant box office success. This was good for the British Film Industry and particularly good news for the town of Scarborough. We could have done with some of the success of the film filtering its way into the Football Club.

Towards the end of the month Paul Ingle and all of Scarborough got the news they had been wanting and waiting for. After a bit of shadow boxing and the usual money wrangling between both fighters' management teams, it was finally on. Paul would fight Prince Naseem at the N.E.C. in Manchester in April. Could Paul turn his European crown into a World crown? Could he bring a World Championship crown back to Scarborough? He was ready for the challenge. Everyone in Scarborough had faith. Tickets would be in high demand. Everyone you talked to was going to give Paul their support. Bring on the Prince. Crown the Yorkshire Hunter!

Earlier in the Season, due to the disruptions and turmoil which beset the Club during the changeover, or intended changeover, a group of ardent supporters rallied together and decided to assist the Club in raising funds and other helpful ventures. They were to be called the Friends of Scarborough Football Club' And more than friends they were. The McCain Lounge which had its roof cave in a few months before, thus causing, amongst other things, much-missed revenue to the Club, would be revamped by the Good Samaritans.

The McCain Lounge was used midweek to bring in finance to the Club. It was used as a bar and for private functions. Recently, it had been unused due to its state of disrepair. This was denying the Club essential income and clearly the renovation and re-opening of the Lounge was very important. The place, shamefully, was becoming a bit of an eyesore and it was sad to see it deteriorate.

The Lounge was in drastic need of a complete overhaul and refurbishment. The Friends put out a challenge that they could completely renovate the McCain Lounge inside the space of a weekend. A tall order, even by Anneka Rice's standards! Surely it couldn't be done in a month let alone a weekend?

They managed to beg, steal and borrow everything. They managed somehow to acquire the skill of local tradesmen and the charity of local businesses to supply all that was necessary. This is what community spirit is all about. It is situations like this that makes you proud to be connected to Scarborough Football Club and which gives you the drive and desire to give all these people what they want most in their lives. A successful football team.

As the team left to go to Southend on the Saturday morning, work had been going on through the previous night. The Lounge was like Hiroshima when we left! It was as if an atomic bomb had been dropped on the place. We thought, as we left for Southend, that the chance of the McCain Lounge being completely refurbished by the Millennium, let alone the end of the weekend was about as likely as the Pope going to a Rave in Ibiza.

Miraculously, the following Monday a miracle of biblical stature had been performed. The McCain Lounge had been totally gutted, transformed and renewed. It was unbelievable to see. The place was fit for royalty. O.K., maybe Joe Royle, but it was tremendous what had been achieved. The McCain Lounge was ready to open again to the public. Ready to bring in the Club some much needed cash. Ready for anything from race nights to Wedding Receptions. It was very impressive and everyone took their caps off to the enthusiasm, endeavour and effort of everyone involved. I don't think such action would be deemed necessary at your Manchester Uniteds and your Liverpools and Arsenals but this is life in the third division and this is what keeps small Clubs like ours afloat. God Bless the Friends.

Southend United were not, it must be said, going through a purple patch. They were struggling in the lower half of the league. Admittedly, not in the pits like us, but not far off. The atmosphere of the place suggested a certain disharmony. The fans were edgy and not altogether behind the team. Alvin Martin was the brunt of much unsavoury chanting from the home fans. Surely football managers don't need to be subjected to such tirades of abuse. They are only human after all and even football managers have feelings!

We started brightly and were unfortunate not to go into the lead. There didn't appear to be any signs of uncertainty and lack of confidence. We were looking good. We controlled the game in key areas and

We will be back

certainly didn't look like a team struggling in the fight to stave off relegation.

Typical of a team in trouble, after playing reasonably well and creating several good goalscoring opportunities, just when we thought we would be returning to Scarborough with a hard-earned, hard-fought away point, we found ourselves trailing 0-1 in the 83rd minute, after conceding a weak goal. We gave the ball away cheaply in our defensive third, failed to cut out the cross and paid the ultimate price. It was one of the very few forays on our goal but it cost us a very valuable point.

There was to be no way back for us. That goal cost us the game. That is the way life is when teams are going through a bad patch. It just takes one piece of misfortune and the losing streak gets longer and winning seems that little bit harder. It was a cruel moment for us. One which we did not deserve on the day. So little problem had been caused. We had coped with any small threat that had arisen and we had shown good composure and patience.

We had created numerous chances, but our biggest chance came right at the death when our on-loan striker, Chris Greenacre, was slipped through with only the goalkeeper to beat and the poor boy wanted the ground to open up and swallow him when he missed a gilt-edged chance to give us a precious point. Would this be a point which could mean so much on May the 8th?

Chris was an honest, hard-working boy and he carried that miss on his young shoulders all the way home. I remember him close to tears as he disembarked from the bus. Apologising to all and sundry as he bade his farewell. But it was back to Scarborough without a point to show for our troubles. Another long, quiet trip back to the East Coast.

Football is a very intense game. The highs and lows are incredible. There is nothing else like them. The depth of emotions are immense. To control the intensity of the game is not always easy. It can make you feel on top of the World or it can make you feel you have been to Hell and back. People often talk of what a fabulous life being a footballer is. Yes, when times are good it is a great life. But, when times are bad it can be a heavy burden to carry. The players of Scarborough Football Club were not experiencing the highs of football. They were very much dealing with difficult times. The burden was heavy on many at the Club.

Our next game was at home to Exeter City. Little did we know it was to be Mick Wadsworth's last home game as manager of Scarborough Football Club. Mick was ready to venture to pastures new. Our first home fixture of the New Year, 1999, and how we longed for form similar to the start of 1998, when we went from the beginning of the year until the end of the Season without losing at home. Our only home defeat being at the hands of Torquay in the play-offs.

It was a victorious start and it provided Mick with his last victory as manager of our Club. He would soon be travelling much further down the East side of the country. Alex Marinkov scored from the penalty spot to seal the win. Could we now set off on a roll and achieve home form like we achieved at the beginning of 1998? It was a very satisfying result and one which we hoped would be repeated regularly between now and May.

On the following Monday Neil Campbell finally said his goodbyes to the Club. He was leaving the McCain Stadium to join Southend United. The deal would bring the Club £15,000 and give Neil the opportunity to develop as a young player at another Club. Neil had been finding it extremely difficult to deliver the promise he had shown towards the end of last Season and decided that a move would enhance his chances of discovering his confidence and goalscoring ability again. He had done well for the Club. Neil was a smashing young man and everyone wished him well with his future.

Shortly after this it was hinted that Hibernian had expressed an interest in our Gaelic Centre Back, Alex Marinkov. Alex was one of the successes of the new signings and had become a big favourite with the fans. We needed quality players. Alex was a quality player and if allowed to go he would be sadly missed. Alex did go and he was sadly missed.

It seemed like rats leaving a sinking ship. There were lots of people departing from the Club but not too many new faces appearing. We needed fresh blood. A new impetus to spark vital life back into the Club.

Dave Bassett became the first managerial casualty of 1999 when he was sacked by Nottingham Forest. A few months previous the Club's Dutch star Pierre Van Hooijdonk walked out on the Club claiming the Club lacked ambition after they sold his strike partner Kevin Campbell. He eventually returned when the Club were in a deep relegation battle. Bassett learned his fate on his car radio as he drove to the ground. Bassett said, 'Van Hooijdonk destroyed me. He's still at the Club. I'm not. I've gone because he was a bigger investment than me'. There was a massive amount of sympathy for Dave Bassett and his stand against Van Hooijdonk.

There are varied views on the value and benefit of the foreign influx into our game. Van Hooijdonk and Fabrizzio Ravanelli had done nothing to enhance the reputation of the overseas footballer. They had more than greatly hindered and harmed the name of the European footballer. They had respectively let down their clubs, their managers, their fellow professionals and the clubs' supporters. I don't think Dave Bassett will swoop too readily to purchase from abroad in the future. More likely, like the British farmer recommends, to buy British!

Mick's last Football League game in charge was at Brighton and Hove Albion. The game would be played at the home of Gillingham. Brighton having to sell the 'Big Issue' as one of the 'homeless' football clubs. Their fans desperate to return to their roots and back where they belonged. Back playing their football in Brighton.

It was shortly to be the end of Mick's reign at Scarborough Football Club. It finished with a 0-1 defeat. A few days later we went to Wigan in the Auto Windscreens Shield. It was to be our last stab at a trip to Wembley. We got trounced 0-3. Mick had decided he could do no more. He felt it was best for everyone that it was time to hear a fresh voice. A new man may provide a new beginning. Mick said his goodbyes to everyone and moved on to Colchester United.

Talk about out of the frying pan into the fire! They were fighting for their lives in the second division. Factions of the fans, as in most cases, stated their points of view. Good riddance. He should have gone long ago. He's put the Club where it is now. He's jumped ship etc.

Were they right? Everyone has their opinion. The facts are that Mick Wadsworth brought many qualities to our Club. He took us to the play-offs and he had brought some quality players to our Club. However, we were now where we were and Mick was the man who was in charge of the side that was battling for Football League survival. Football supporters have very short memories.

On a personal note I was sad to see Mick leave. It was probably the right decision for him but, nonetheless, it was sad to see him go. Mick and I had our differences on occasion but I very much admired many attributes of the man. Mick, for me, is one of the most honest men you could wish to meet. If he didn't like you. He told you. If he hurt you it didn't matter, he did so honestly. If he trusted you he was fiercely loyal.

As Mick moved out, the Chairman acted very quickly. Within days of Mick's departure it was decided that Derek Mountfield and Ray McHale would take charge of first team affairs with Jamie Hoyland and John Kay acting as a players' committee in team selection!

It seemed strange. It was strange. A case of too many chiefs and not enough Indians. It was clear that it was a recipe that wouldn't work and it

We will be back

was very quickly altered. On the first Saturday of the new regime we took an almighty pasting at Glanford Park. We were bludgeoned 1-5 by Scunthorpe. It was a massive defeat and the panic bells were ringing. Again we had taken a miserable three points from another month. We were now one point ahead of Hull City and six points behind Hartlepool. We were in the sixth month of the Season and except for the healthy month of September the Season had been a Season of sickness. Surely it couldn't be a terminal illness?

I think a few people at Scunthorpe that day uttered that they had just played the team that would be playing in the Nationwide Conference next Season. We couldn't blame them. We had let ourselves down. We played with a lack of discipline. A lack of shape and ideas and looked like a team searching for hope. Things were looking decidedly bleak. Scunthorpe looked a league above us. They were streets ahead on the day and on that showing, major surgery was required.

We had taken three points from the month of August. Two points from October, three from November, December and January. We were deep in a dogfight of survival. The management knew it. The players knew it. The fans knew it. The town knew it. The message was clear to see. If we didn't turn things around, and quickly, we would lose our Football League status. God forbid.

11

Too many chiefs, not enough indians

FEBRUARY 1999

At a time when Derek was setting out on the hazardous road of management, the National Coach, Glenn Hoddle was coming to the end of his reign. It was announced early in the month that Glenn was giving up the post of England manager due to comments he had made about handicapped people and reincarnation.

At one time managers would only be relieved of their post if they were not achieving the required results on the football pitch. Those days had long gone. It is now the days of high profile. Especially if you were the England team manager. Everything, but everything, gets scrutinised if you are the National supremo. Look at Hoddle's poor predecessors. They were almost crucified by the Press. Glenn Hoddle would be spared no leniency.

There was no way back. Glenn Hoddle offered his resignation and was England manager no more. His reign had been brief. Ended prematurely. His record had been unmemorable and his reputation had been destroyed. A job which many consider the dream post had again been a living nightmare for another ex-England boss. Would he be able to salvage his reputation in the future or was the England job the job that finished the very promising managerial career of Glenn Hoddle?

In the following days the papers were saturated with suitable candidates. Glenn had barely got his feet out of 16 Lancaster Gate and already his successor was being suggested by the tabloid team management experts. Those literary geniuses who extol to the Nation there can be only one real choice, then when he has been elected, begin to verbally castrate him in the months that follow.

It wasn't too long after that the F. A. appointed the peoples' choice, Kevin Keegan. They had put Howard Wilkinson, their Technical Director, in charge for a brief spell but quickly gave the job to K. K., albeit on a temporary basis. This is what everybody wanted. Kevin was the man for the job. He is Mr. Charisma itself. He is the man to give the players the belief. He is the man to make England great again.

Kevin didn't want the job on a full-time basis. He wanted to run it in conjunction with his managerial post at Fulham! A little ludicrous you may say but if anyone could combine the two posts then King Kevin was the man.

Prior to Kevin's appointment the National side took on the newly crowned kings of World football, France at Wembley Stadium. Howard Wilkinson as Technical Director of English football would select and take control of the team. Not an easy baptism! England were no match for the champions of the World and were beaten comprehensively 0-2. Two goals being expertly taken by the young Arsenal striker Nicolas Anelka and a game which was orchestrated by the magic of Zidane. It takes a good side to beat England at Wembley. The French are a good side.

Derek Mountfield was very new to the role of management and what a baptism he inherited. There would be no combination of jobs for Derek. He wouldn't be taking over a team of super-confidents. He inherited a team suffering in lack of confidence. Players who did not know where their next win was coming from and a Club without the resources to buy change. Derek had had more than his fair share of success as a player. He had been there, seen it, done it and got the T shirt. Championship medals and European triumphs were in his locker. Management is a different ball game. Derek had no previous experience. No record to judge. But, Derek was ready for the challenge.

Over the course of the Season, possibly due to the torrid run of results, players' beliefs were at an all time low. There was not too much sign of positive talk around the place and, if the truth was known, relegation was written on the faces of some of the players. Time was running out and a change of attitude was essential. An injection of confidence and direction was essential.

Derek and Ray instantly planned the way forward. Derek hadn't experienced much failure in his time as a player and he was determined his

We will be back

managerial career would follow the same path of success. Ray had great knowledge of life in the lower divisions and would provide Derek with the direction that was necessary to climb the table away from the trap door to doom. It appeared to be a good combination.

They needed time, but time was short. Ascendancy had to happen sooner than later. Very quickly they set about rectifying the need for change. Almost every night one or 'tother, if not both, were taking in a game. They were selective in the games they viewed. They had to be. They had no money to spend. We were lying on the precipice of the Conference and the attraction of Scarborough Football Club to a Football League player was not exactly something they would drool over. Infact, I think some players would have found the visit to a leper colony more attractive than signing their names to Scarborough Football Club!

Derek and Ray worked tirelessly for the Club, and as time would tell, they performed minor miracles. Their commitment to the cause was magnificent as they set about their quest to achieve Football League security.

On the first Saturday in February we played Cambridge at home. They were flying. We were dying. The games were coming but they weren't coming easy. This was a tough fixture. Like Scunthorpe. We could have done with a team out of form, with a team that wasn't battling for promotion. But a team that was sitting pretty in the middle of the league without any chance of promotion or relegation. Cambridge were fighting for promotion. They needed to beat us. After all the footballing experts had tipped an away victory and an away win is what they expected. They got it, in comfort. With ease.

We were banjoed 1-5, steam-rollered, and were appalling on the day. The fans who attended that day could not possibly like what they had seen. No matter how loyal they may be to their beloved team this defeat must have left a bitter taste in the mouth. We looked like a team void of ideas. A team deep in the mire and a team that the fans would find difficulty in remaining loyal in their support.

The second 1-5 hammering in a row. Ten goals conceded in two games. How could the fans accept this. Fans also have their pride in their team and this latest butchering must have made them embarrassed to be a Seasider. I remember thinking as many of them made their exit from the Stadium way before the final whistle was sounded that it may be the last time we see some of those fans in this Season of need. Nonetheless, the battle for survival would continue and the towel would not be thrown in.

Derek and Ray had again been busy during the week leading up to the

Cambridge game. They knew they needed fresh bodies. They knew they needed an injection of optimism. They knew they needed a front player. Chris Greenacre was coming to the end of his loan period and they felt Chris was not the player who could answer the call of survival. He was not the man to give us the goals which would give us the gift of remaining in the Football League. He was a young man learning his trade. We needed something different. We needed the finished article.

Darren Roberts was seen to be that man. Darren was brought in from Darlington and instantly thrown into the fight for survival.

Darren relished the opportunity of first team football. He had been a fringe player at Darlington and wanted a piece of the action. There was no bedding in for new players. It was frontline straight away. Darren was thrown into the trenches and was expected to fight to win the war. He was a fighter. He would certainly stand up and be counted.

In all our home games since we entered the Football League in Season 1987/1988 this was to be the biggest home defeat experienced. The defeat

The very popular Darren Roberts celebrating with Michael 'The Beast' McNaughton one of his goals for Scarborough

We will be back

to Cambridge. Derek had introduced his first new face and was scouring the division for more. There would be no hiding place. No place for shirkers. It was all hands to the pumps and stronger resolve required.

After the annihilation to Cambridge Derek called a team meeting and everything was discussed. The non-believers could go. There was no place for self-pity. Mental strength and character was what was vital. If you played with fear you could go, and quickly. There was much talk, positive talk and little negativity to be heard. We would survive and don't doubt it. This was the message that had to be sounded and this was the message the players needed to hear.

The following Saturday we made the long trek to Shrewsbury. It was no overnight stay for us. This Club could not afford the luxury of a good nights sleep and a long lie in before an important match. It was an early start. A tiring trip and a late arrival. Hardly the preparation for players desperate to maintain their credibility and Football League status. We had come off the back of two 1-5 embarrassments, Six away defeats on the bounce and no glimmer of winning a game.

We had to stem the tide of defeat and conclude this lengthening period of despair. Victories had to be found. Points had to be taken and respectability had to be restored. Everyone was determined but it would not be found easily.

We went down 1-3. Seven away defeats on the bounce but, we had seen something from this game which hadn't been evident before. A glimmer of hope appeared. We had played with passion. We had created chances and defended soundly for large parts of the game. We had been beaten but the atmosphere was different in the dressing room. The players came off with their heads held high. On many previous occasions they were down by their knees. They felt the wind of change blow. A genuine optimism was evident.

The following week Ray and Derek were out searching for new talent. Two new players were brought to the McCain Stadium. Ray had watched Graeme Atkinson in a reserve match at Scunthorpe and was so impressed that he instantly recommended him to Derek and he was added to the playing staff hastily. Also introduced was Gary Porter from Walsall. A Seasoned pro with much Football League experience. Both played in our next home match against Swansea.

With new faces came new faith. The new arrivals hadn't come for the glory. Nor had they come to be remembered as being one of the squad who lost their Football League status. Their freshness was clearly evident in training and around the Club. They visibly lifted some of the players who had previously been stuck in the rut of relegation. They were part of what was desperately needed.

The positive vibes from the Shrewsbury game were justified. The team, with its new boys played with conviction and style. Graeme Atkinson had a magnificent debut, playing like Roberto Carlos. With Brazilian flair and fire. The new strike partnership of Chris Tate and Darren Roberts were like Keegan and Toshack. They were superb, each scoring a goal and playing as if they had played together forever. A 2-1 victory. A win with style, confidence and commitment. It wasn't too late. We could turn the whole Season on its head and finish with a flourish.

The new management team of McHale and Mountfield had earned their first taste of victory. Little did they know it would be their last. Up in the stand that Saturday afternoon sat Colin Addison. Colin was there as a guest of the Chairman. Colin was there to watch over the team he was about to manage. Derek's reign of manager was to be over before it really

Graeme Atkinson - Boro's influential wing back in action against our North East neighbours Darlington.

We will be back

began. The team would have its third manager inside six weeks.

Colin had managed at the very top, and the very bottom. His experience was vast. From the giants of Athletico Madrid to the minnows of Merthyr. He had been there. He had been out of management for a while and the last thing he expected was to be back in the pit of pressure again.

Colin was outside his Hereford home, just about to pack his golf clubs, ready to visit the local golf course and play a round with one of his golfing friends when the telephone sounded in his home. His wife Jean took the call and informed Colin that Kevin Green from Scarborough Football Club was wanting to speak to him.

'Kevin Green from Scarborough?' he said to Jean. He didn't know Kevin Green from Scarborough.

The conversation was short. Kevin informed Colin Scarborough wanted to speak to him about managing the side. Colin wasn't interested. He didn't want to go through the rigmaroll of interviews and no thank yous. The thank you for attending routine. We'll let you know. There was to be no interview. Did he want the job? If he did the job was his. He would be the new manager of Scarborough Football Club.

From the stand that Saturday Colin witnessed his future team deliver a three point performance. He wanted the job. He got it, and was announced as the new team manager. It all happened so speedily. Colin was thrust into the fight for survival. He was ready for the challenge.

It was all change again at the helm. Colin was the new supremo and the partnership of Ray and Derek had been relinquished. They had worked extremely hard in the weeks previous and their efforts had gone unrecognised. The Board had decided change was necessary and that although they wished Derek and Ray to remain very much involved with the Coaching Staff and in managerial decisions they wanted Colin to be the man giving all the appropriate actions to lead us to survival.

The F. A. Cup was now well under way and in the middle of this month the fifth round was held. There was to be no real giant-killing upsets but there was to be an amazing incident at Highbury in the match between Arsenal and Sheffield United.

With the game locked at 1-1 and in its final stages a Sheffield United player needed treatment. The ball was kicked out of play. It had been waiting to happen. This moment of fairplay when the opposition are meant to return the ball to the team who had kicked the ball out, did not return the ball to them. Arsenal threw the ball back into play but Marc Overmars and Khanu had not read the script and proceeded to put Arsenal 2-1 up and win the game.

Immediately after the game, Arsene Wenger astounded the football world by stating that he wished the game to be replayed. He did not want victory in this manner. It was an unacceptable method of victory for Arsenal Football Club. The F. A. supported this view, sanctioned a replay, and an amazing precedent was set. Arsenal put Sheffield United out of the Competition, a few days later, in a way that was acceptable to Arsene Wenger!

In a Season where much disrepute had been displayed this was a refreshing breath of fairplay and one which had to be admired in these days of football pressures. Arsene Wenger and Arsenal Football Club deserved rich praise for this very sporting gesture and showed football up in its true light.

Colin's first game at the helm was away to Brentford. Not an easy place to start. We had beaten them brilliantly at our place earlier in the Season but they were no soft touches and they were looking like automatic promotion candidates. They were going particularly well and would show no sentiment towards our new manager. We had to be prepared.

During the week we had managed to sign the very experienced Tony Parks. Tony gave us that wealth of experience in goal which we had lacked since the unfortunate Tony Elliot had injured his back. Tony would give us that authoritative voice from behind the defence which we had lacked for some time. Tony would also bring his personality into a dressing room which was searching for inspiration.

We got a richly deserved 1-1 draw with our young striker Chris Tate getting his third goal in four games. It was the kind of away point that had been sadly lacking for most of the Season and a big point to salvage from the trip to the capital. It was a big night and a big result.

We had taken four points from the last six. It was only the third time in the Season we had gone two games unbeaten and the first time since October. We were still firmly rooted to the bottom of the table as the month of February closed its curtains. We were five points adrift of Hull City but the wind of change was blowing.

12

Hope springs eternal

MARCH 1999

The month of March was meant to start with a home game against Plymouth but due to the inclement weather our game was postponed. We wanted it on. We were on a mini run. In fact a minuscule run! Two games unbeaten. It wasn't quite the run of epic proportions that Manchester United go on regularly, but it was a run, and we wanted it to continue. But the game couldn't have been played. Not for the first time this Season the pitch was awash. There was an air of frustration but it gave Colin time to reflect, to take stock, and to make plans.

The North of England had received some of its heaviest rainfall for many, many years. Many rivers had burst their banks and much havoc was to be found. The local countryside around Scarborough was akin to a giant lake. Farmers' fields were no longer farmers' fields. They were totally submerged. Trees which normally stood high in all their glory were barely able to peak out above the flood. It was quite incredible. I kind of half expected to see Noah's Ark sail down Scarborough way.

Needless to say, every possible area of grass was waterlogged and incapable of providing a surface for football. Possibly a ski-jetter, but certainly not a footballer. At a time like this Scarborough has the great fortune of being beside the Seaside. And, the only place where it is humanly possible to acquire a surface, which can provide footballers with a surface to play on, is on the beach. That's if the tide is out. Not so good if the tide is in!

Training was affected but at least we could still do some outdoor work. Colin was able to structure a training programme which minimised the inconvenience caused by the incessant rainfall we had undergone. The beach is often used as another training option. Some people cruelly said it was the best place for our team to play as we were a bunch of donkeys anyway!

Colin instantly endeared himself to everyone. He is a noble man, morally sound. A man of principle and a man of trust. He epitomised honesty and displayed not a hint of aloofness. He had time for everyone and everyone was equal. He made no promises. He gave no false hopes. He gave only the words that if he did not succeed it would not be for the want of trying.

It became clear from the beginning that Colin was very much on the side of his players. He is a player's manager. If he could do anything to assist the welfare of his players nothing was too much trouble.

Some managers are accused of having no time for their players and only interested in themselves. Not so with Colin. He made it clear that his door was always open to his players and if they had any problems he was there to listen and to help.

Colin's next game in charge was a visit to Chester City. We had never won there before. We stopped for a pre-match just outside Chester and the atmosphere in the camp was good. Players were relaxed and the signs were good. After eating we had a briefing and Colin informed players of their responsibilities. Who were the threats and where we could get some joy. The preparation was thorough.

From the hotel we made the short journey to the Diva Stadium. It was a lovely, calm evening and the conditions were excellent for football. Little wind, nice pitch with a bit of moisture on the grass to provide a surface which would enable the ball to move with a bit of zip. Just the way footballers like it.

That evening the new potent partnership of Roberts and Tate up front were on form again with Chris Tate scoring a brace and taking his goal tally to five goals in five games. Matthew Russell scored a late third to give us a 3-1 victory. A goal which was missed by his father, the Chairman, John Russell.

John regularly missed large parts of matches as his tension tended to get the better of him. John put the wreck into nervous. He is passionate about his football. He is more than the Chairman. He is a passionate fan. He kicks every ball, well, every ball that he sees!

We will be back

Miss his son's goal he did but he was in the dressing room at the end to congratulate everyone for such an important away win. It was a great win. Our third game unbeaten and seven points from nine. The teams above us were now starting to get within touching distance and we were determined to give the ignominy of bottom place to someone else. We had spent too long where we did not belong.

As we made our way away from the Diva Stadium we were all working out possible scenarios to the way the remainder of the Season would go. Who would win which games. Who would go on a downward spiral. Which team would go on a run and which team would ultimately wave goodbye to the Football League. There was much debate. There were many views but everyone was unanimous, Scarborough were staying up.

For David Beckham, it was becoming not an Annus Horriblis as everyone expected after his moment of madness in France, but a fantastic year. His footballing career was going swimmingly and, in this month he became the proud father of a baby boy. Little Brooklyn Beckham. I have to be honest and say I'm not convinced about the name. David and Victoria had said they had named the child after the place where the little man was conceived. One radio wag said, thank God he was not conceived in South London or the wee fellow might have been lumbered with the name, Peckham Beckham!

Me being me, I have to say, this is another thing that tends to mystify me. That time when a newly born comes into this beautiful world and his or her parents take leave of their senses and give the poor little sibling the burden of having to carry on their backs for the rest of their lives the most ridiculous name that anyone has ever had to be called. Brooklyn, I'm sure will become a very popular name but I'm not certain it will stand the test of time like good old names such as John and Jack and James.

Not only was David celebrating the birth of his first child he was celebrating qualifying for the European Champions League Semi Final and the F. A. Cup Semi Final with fantastic victories over the Invincible Inter Milan and the charismatic Chelsea, respectively.

United demolished Inter at home 2-0 with both goals coming from their record signing Dwight Yorke. Dwight was making his huge transfer fee look quite insignificant as United cruised towards the Treble. People were now starting to talk about the unachievable treble being achieved.

They followed this up with a comfortable 1-1 draw in Milan. They were closing in on their dream. European Champions League winners. Alex Ferguson had brought them every possible piece of silverware bar the one that really mattered. The one that hung like an albatross around the neck of every Manchester United player since that great night at Wembley in 1968. It was now within touching distance. Could they reach out and grasp it?

After an 0-0 draw against Chelsea they marched onto the Semi Final stage with a 2-0 victory at the hands of Gianluca Vialli's Chelsea. They were now so near but everyone was still convinced they were so far. The big games would come thick and fast. Surely too much for any one team?

In our next match, a home game against Rotherham, we didn't get out of the starting blocks. We were flat and caught Rotherham on a particularly good game for them. After missing a good chance early on we conceded and collapsed to a 0-4 home defeat. It was Colin's first defeat in charge of the side and he was very philosophical in defeat. There were no excuses. No ifs and buts, just brutal honesty. We were second best. Men against boys. Deservedly beaten. End of story. Let's move on !

Exactly the correct response. No time for moping. No time for excuses. No time for panic. We had been comprehensively beaten but it was now a case of rapidly picking ourselves up, dusting ourselves down and getting back on the three point trail.

During this month we saw the departure of one of our bright young stars Richard Jackson. Richard was sold to Premier League Derby County. It was a fantastic move for Richard and it was one which had been predicted by people in the Club long before. Richard was another homegrown player. He had been at the Club since the age of 14 and his talent was there to be seen even from that very young age.

Richard throughout his time at Scarborough conducted himself in the best possible manner. He was liked by everyone and always showed that he had all the attributes necessary to become a Professional footballer.

Everyone was sad to see the end of the Jackson Five at the Club. This was the name we had given to Richard's family as they followed him everywhere. Mother, Father, Granny and two sisters. We all feel he can be the next Denis Irwin. Time will tell. Success couldn't happen to a nicer young man.

In this month football was rocked at the foundations when Chelsea coach, Graham Rix, was sentenced to twelve months in prison for unlawful sex with a fifteen year old schoolgirl.

There was widespread condemnation when Chelsea announced they would remain loyal to their first team coach and that he will receive his old job back when he completes his sentence for the crime he has committed.

We will be back

Rix would be put on a police sex offenders list but he will resume his career at a high profile Premier League Club, such as Chelsea when his sentence has been served. Chelsea feel that he will have been punished for his crime and should be allowed to pick up the pieces of his life and get back to the job he does best, and which Chelsea Football Club feel he should be permitted to do. Not everyone expresses the same view.

Our next two, and last two games in the month of March were against Torquay and Rochdale. The re-arranged fixture from November. We had to make the long trip to Torquay before facing Rochdale at the McCain Stadium. We needed to put Rotherham behind us, and quick. We got a magnificent six points from the two games. This made it thirteen points from a possible eighteen in our last six games. We finished the month on thirty seven points. The same points as Hartlepool, but having played a game less. It had been a brilliant month and gave us all the will to take it on from there.

There was now light at the end of the tunnel. There was a ray of hope. From a position of gloom we had hauled ourselves into a place of possible salvation. It was now up to us to grasp the nettle. Take the bull by the horns and surge on. It had been a valliant effort through this month and with six weeks remaining of the Season destiny was in our hands.

Sandwiched in between the Torquay and Rochdale games was deadline day. After this date no Club could buy, sell or take on loan a player from, or to another Club. Or so we thought. We were busy trying to strengthen our squad and just before five o'clock we managed to acquire the services of Nathan Jones, a cultured left-sided midfield player from Southend. A player who would give us extra cover on the left side and give us a creative midfield addition.

Colin knew Nathan from earlier days and was convinced he could provide us with that bit of balance we needed on the left hand side and that Nathan had the ability to hurt the opposition with his useful left foot.

Carlisle were at the same time selling their number one 'keeper to Blackpool for a minimal payment and taking on loan a young, relatively inexperienced goalkeeper from Derby. This seemed madness to us. We had only recently had two young 'keepers on loan and, as I have already said, they will both become very good goalkeepers in time, they were not the answer to our problem at this moment in time. We wondered if the young 'keeper from Derby could answer the problems that faced Carlisle but we felt we knew the answer.

There is immense pressures on players fighting for their teams' survival and none moreso on a goalkeeper. Especially young goalkeepers with very little games experience at this level. Carlisle were, in our view taking a huge risk. Would they live to regret this strange transaction?

Everyone knows that at times the pressure in football, and in particular, on managers, can be intense. Early in this month football got a big fright when Joe Kinnear, the Wimbledon manager was taken to hospital with a suspected heart attack prior to Wimbledon's game with Sheffield Wednesday.

Wimbledon were riding high in the league and in the Semi Final of the Worthington Cup. It obviously cannot be confirmed that Joe's heart attack can be attached to the pressures of the game but it makes you stop to consider.

Joe's team went out of the Worthington Cup, as he lay in hospital recovering, beaten at the hands of their London rivals Tottenham Hotspur and the first major Competition was settled at Wembley on the 21st March when Tottenham won their first trophy for many years with a 1-0 win against Leicester City. The game was won with what was virtually the last kick of the game, or should I say header, when Allan Neilsen dived to head Tottenham into the record books. George Graham had arrived only months earlier but already he had shown his Midas touch by delivering Spurs their first piece of silverware since 1991.

The Season was heading into the home straight. There were ten games to go and the heat in the kitchen was turning up. It was heading towards April and some crucial matches against other sides struggling in the depths of despair, were to be played. Scarborough, Carlisle and Hartlepool were fighting for their lives. We had hit a purple patch at the right time, now all we needed to do was keep it going and turn it into a golden memory. And a fond wave goodbye to one of the other two sides as they sailed off to the distant shores of the Conference.

13

Rock Bottom

APRIL 1999

April started with the Easter weekend, usually a vital weekend in determining the fortunes of many teams. Who was going to get promotion. Who was heading for relegation. Was another manager due the chop? They are usually weekends of tension and nervousness. We had two games both designed for the man of steel and to be avoided by the marshmallow man.

We had a trip to Boothferry Park on the Saturday and Carlisle were to attend at the McCain Stadium on the Easter Monday. Two teams battling for survival, like ourselves. Crucial games, which would probably give a clearer picture of who was the most likely candidate to face the guillotine. We were determined it would not be us.

This was a rare occurrence for us. To have a home match on a Bank Holiday Monday was normally a no-goer. Seaside resorts, at least Scarborough, could not have the luxury of a home fixture on such days. The town's population was greatly increased by visitors during this period. Accordingly, policing had to be intensified and the demands placed on the local Police Constabulary meant that officers couldn't be spared, to police a football match. Consequently, usually Bank Holiday Mondays meant away travel for us.

In the lead up to this vitally important weekend, calamity struck at the heart of the team. A flu bug hit with a vengeance. So many of our players went down that we were scratching for a side to field. It got so bad that on the Friday the Club had to telephone the Football League and explain our plight. We were requesting the postponement of the Hull City fixture. In no uncertain terms we were told the game would go ahead. If it meant having to field a team consisting of our Youth Team, then that's what we would have to do!

We would have to make sweeping changes for the game ahead. There could be no special dispensation given. If you cannot field professionals, then we must field apprentices. No ifs or buts, this was the Football League's stance and we had to get on with it. If only they had taken this stance at Carlisle!

Hull City had earlier in the Season been cast as virtual certainties for the Conference. They had miraculously turned their Season round and were showing form which, if had been there earlier in the Season, would have made them Division Three champions. They were buzzing. The city was behind them and didn't they show it.

The team arrived at the Posthouse Forte Hotel overlooking the River Humber for a pre-match meal, and, where we would pick up the team bus to take us into Boothferry Park. It was a beautiful Spring morning and there was a calmness about the squad as we made our final preparations for the afternoon's match.

I remember going for a walk with Colin and Ray around the grounds as the players relaxed after their meal watching Football Focus. Colin said he had a good feeling about him. Although things were not nearly perfect with regard to the flu situation and players now having to be asked to get themselves out of their sick beds and fight for the cause, he felt the players would respond. We knew this was going to be one of the toughest games we would have to face all Season, but Colin felt we would rise to the occasion.

Colin in his final talk with the players at the Hotel, informed the players of their responsibilities, their debt to the supporters and to salvage their personal pride. He had every faith in them. He wanted them to have faith in themselves. It was going to be an intimidating atmosphere. A hostile atmosphere. An afternoon for the brave. He told the players to be brave. We were now in the eleventh round of the fight, we could still win on points.

Today was a vitally important day in the history of Scarborough Football Club. It was also a vitally important day in the lives of two young newly-weds who were having their reception at the Hotel. They arrived at

We will be back

the Hotel as we were departing. The players and management stopped to applaud them and wish them every success in their future lives together. Although they were young man and wife from Hull they wished us every good luck in the match ahead.

As the team bus made its way from the Hotel through the streets of Hull and into Boothferry Park we could see the place was buzzing. There were fans everywhere as we neared the Stadium. I remember, as we approached into the Car Park at the front of the ground, seeing a couple of our young Centre of Excellence players bedecked in their Scarborough Centre of Excellence tracksuits. It was two young boys who were actually from Hull but today their young hearts were very much with Scarborough.

We arrived at Boothferry Park in good time and we expected a good atmosphere for the game. We were not disappointed. The place was bursting at the seems. Nearly 14,000 fans were present. It was unbelievable for two teams in the dungeons of the league to attract such a following. It was a big game for both teams. The fixture had produced the biggest crowd in Division Three this Season. Hopefully, we could repeat this occasion again next year.

This was the first time for many of our players that they had played in front of such a big crowd. They certainly had been used to performing in front of much lesser crowds this Season. Infact it was a standing joke that there was sometimes more people fitted into a Bobsleigh than were at our games. Not so today, the place was bouncing. As the players were conducting their warm up, the audience were conducting their vocal chord warm up. The singing and chanting was fantastic.

Prior to the game I spoke with Rod Arnold, the Hull City Youth Team manager. He had said it had been a hair-raising Season at the Club. At one point he felt that it would be his Club that would be going down. Things were now different. He felt confident Hull would stay up. We both agreed we wanted neither to go down. The two Clubs were good for each other in the league. Close neighbours, healthy rivalry and above all two Clubs who liked each other.

When the teams came out the noise just smacked you in the face and it was the kind of atmosphere that you want to taste more often. It made the hairs on the back of your neck stand on end. The April sun shone high up above. The sky was cloudless and the heat was intense. The heat of the occasion.

The game did not disappoint, with both teams going at it hammer and tong to get maximum points. The spectators were in full cry. The football provided encouraged the fan to sing and chant louder than the person next to them. The first forty five was full of goal mouth incident and chances. The two teams weren't here for a point, they were both fighting for three.

The half time whistle sounded. Nobody heard it as the noise was deafening, but eventually the officials got the message across. It was a half of intensity and commitment. The players could now get a moment to recover, the coaching staff could give crucial guidance and the fans could recharge their vocal chords!

We felt we had played the better football in the team discussion at half time and that we must carry the performance forward in the second half. We mustn't get careless, lose our discipline or concentration and undo all the good work we had done in the first forty five minutes. We felt we could cause an aerial threat to the Hull defence. It was important we worked the ball into wide areas and delivered crosses which would create problems to the home rear-guard. We must be conscious of the threat of Brabin and not allow him space in and around the box.

Through the week prior we had discussed the threat Gary Brabin would pose. He was a very robust player who created a big threat with his aerial qualities. He had to be watched. He had been watched until a ball was delivered in from the Hull right flank and Brabin rose to fire in a powerful header to open the scoring and put Hull ahead. The place went bananas. The home side had taken the lead and the visitors were in their place.

Colin instructed calm to his players and to continue to play with spirit and belief. Regularly he talked about good and bad times during football matches and the need to cope with them. This was one of those difficult periods. We required composure and purpose. This we did and late in the game we got our just reward. A corner kick from the left was met by a Jamie Hoyland header and the scoreline was level. We had done it. It was a massive away point. It was a great psychological boost to everyone. We had shown great resolve and the spirit in the squad was buoyant.

In the changing room Colin thanked the players for their gallant efforts and praised them on their mental strength to overcome a 1-0 deficit in front of a very partisan home support. They had richly deserved their point and he reminded them there was another mammoth game on Monday. Be sensible. Have a well-earned drink, but don't over-indulge. Rest and be ready at three o'clock Monday.

After the game Ray and I loaded the skips on to the Club's minibus and set off on the short journey back to Scarborough. No luxury coaches for us.

We will be back

No time to stop for a post-match drink. This was Scarborough Football Club and this was the mode of transport for the day.

As we made our return to Scarborough from Hull Ray and I reflected on the day. The spirit of the side under such a hostile atmosphere. The bottle the players had shown after spending most of the week laid low through illness. The desire and determination to salvage something from the game when we found ourselves 0-1 down in the second half and the patience shown in grinding out an equaliser.

The conversation was full of predictions and permutations. If we do this and they do that we could finish with this and they could finish with that. It was one of those confabs that don't really solve anything but are so very common amongst football people. One thing it did reinforce was our absolute belief that we would survive. It had been a demanding day but a very gratifying one for all of us.

On the Monday it was another relegation battle against Carlisle. Carlisle were now down in the mess and were looking decidedly edgy in their recent showings. We were again three games unbeaten and looking to extend it to four. Confidence was high and we felt as if we couldn't be beaten. It was a feeling, a good feeling, that hadn't been too prominent throughout the Season.

It was a vital weekend and Colin insisted in everything being meticulously planned. The players who lived outside the town, were asked to come to Scarborough on the Sunday evening and stay overnight in the Club's hotel. Thus avoiding the possibility of huge delays due to the Bank Holiday Monday traffic. This was to prove very sensible indeed.

Carlisle United duly got caught up in the thick traffic coming into Scarborough on the Bank Holiday Monday and found themselves very short of time between arrival and kick off. They were a little irritated to say the least and this infuriating delay would possibly be a contributory factor in their team's poor performance on the day.

We had got our first Bank Holiday home fixture for what seemed like years. We wanted a big crowd, both for the revenue and the atmosphere. It was a lovely Spring afternoon, and if the crowds didn't show today, then they would never show.

The roads into Scarborough were bursting with Bank Holiday traffic. The town was always amass with visitors eager to enjoy a day by the seaside. Scarborough was very popular on such holidays. We hoped a large amount of the visitors would be making their way to the McCain Stadium to see this huge game for both Scarborough and Carlisle.

We will be back

Jamie Hoyland, scorer of Boro's crucial equaliser against Hull City

Over 3,000 attended. It was our biggest home crowd of the Season. A win was vital for both teams. It was said that the young 'keeper Carlisle had taken on deadline day was finding it difficult to deal with the situation he found himself in. He was the last line of defence in a team that was suffering and was said to be a little suspect. We discussed getting at him quickly and as often as possible. We couldn't afford to make life any easier for him.

We will be back

Chris Tate was electric on the day. He played with sophistication, maturity, and scored three, clinically taken goals in a 3-0 win. The first player in a Boro' shirt to do this since Darren Foreman. Chris had now taken his goal ratio to eight goals in ten games and was forming a formidable frontline partnership with Darren Roberts. We deserved all three points and we sensed that we had struck a big moral blow to Carlisle. Was this the team destined for the Conference?

As the Carlisle players and management departed from the Stadium they looked like a team which had accepted the inevitable. They looked totally, dejected, dispirited, down-trodden and the journey back to Carlisle would be a long and painful one for them.

We had taken four points in three big days. We knew the importance of these two matches and we responded magnificently. We had dealt Carlisle a massive blow and we did not succumb to the pressure put on us at Hull. We had to be very satisfied with our weekends work.

We had now taken ten points from twelve and only experienced one defeat since Colin took over at the helm. Was he proving to be our King Midas? What had brought about this remarkable change to the Club? Was it Colin? Had it been the foundation laid by Derek Mountfield before? Was it the introduction of the new personnel? Was it the introduction of our young Y. T. S. player Shaun Rennison to the fold? Everyone had their views.

Since Renno's appearance at Shrewsbury he had become an ever-present. For one so young he was displaying a great maturity. Unaffected by the situation. If anything thriving in the pressure. He had been a rock at the back. Stifling many attacks and commanding in the air. Against Carlisle Shaun suffered an injury which would keep him out of the side for the next four matches. It was to prove a costly absence.

Easter weekends so often make or break teams. It can be the short period of time, three days, when Championships can be decided. When relegation can be settled and the Season is all but over. The Easter weekend had been very good for us. It bridged the gap, gave us hope and left us with complete optimism that we could escape the big drop.

Meanwhile at the Merseyside derby Robbie Fowler brought the game into disrepute with a stupid act of simulating drug taking after scoring against Everton. This was the second time Robbie had been charged with misconduct following his confrontation with Graeme Le Saux in their recent match with Chelsea. Robbie was fined £32,000 and given a six match suspension, effectively ending his Season. On Robbie's own admission he had behaved appallingly and warranted the action taken by the

We will be back

Football Association. Robbie is a player of immense promise. He will have time to reflect, to take stock and decide his future. I hope he fulfils all his potential.

April was a busy month for Scarborough Football Club. We had seven games to play. We had taken four points from the first two. It had been a great Easter for us. We would take no more points from the remaining five games in the month of April! Calamity. All of a sudden we nose-dived. The brakes went on and we tumbled downhill fast. Easter quickly became a forgotten time of optimism and promise.

It was devastating, no points from five games. From a position of relative safety we hit the wall. The clouds opened and the bubble burst. We lost to Barnet, Darlington and Hartlepool. On the evening of the Barnet game most of Scarborough came to a standstill to watch the heroic performance given by the Yorkshire Hunter, Paul Ingle, in his quest to take Prince Naseem's World title.

He came very close to causing a major upset. In the tenth round it looked as if Paul was going to do the unthinkable and stop the Prince. He had him wobbling. Alas, it was not to be. In the next round he got caught by a Prince bomb and it was goodnight Vienna. Paul had done himself proud and all of Scarborough were so appreciative of his gutsy performance.

We then played Leyton Orient on the Wednesday of the 21st. One Thousand, four hundred fans attended. We had changed our midweek matches to Wednesdays thinking it would attract more fans. We didn't account for Manchester United having an incredible run in Europe.

That night, United were at the San Siro playing in the second leg of the European Champions League Semi Final. They had drawn at Old Trafford 1-1 and needed to score to get to that elusive European Champions Final which had lived in the dreams of every United fan since that magnificent night at Wembley in '68.

We lost our fourth game on the spin, going down 1-3. The atmosphere at the game was non-existent. There was more noise to be heard in the town's graveyard. It was a pathetic attendance. How could we expect to attract fans down to the McCain Stadium on a night when Manchester United could reach their Holy Grail? They were on the verge of a historic triple. We were on the verge of anonymity. Scarborough people decided to be armchair fans that evening. And who could blame them. As much as we needed them at this critical hour, they stayed at home and gave the McCain Stadium a wide berth.

We will be back

The Chairman was so down-heartened by the lack of support. We were fighting for our lives and we needed all hands on deck. This included a support to show the players they were playing for a Club and a town who cared. It appeared to him that it was a town that didn't care. He had aired these views often in the past. It has to be said, with justification and he would air them again.

Just one week before United reached the final of the F. A. Cup with a 2-1 win over their arch-rivals Arsenal, with the winner coming from a wonder goal off the trusted left boot of Ryan Giggs. A goal that will be talked about for years to come. Tonight, they found themselves 0-2 down after a mere eleven minutes courtesy of two goals from Juventus's lethal striker Inzaghi. United were on the brink of defeat when they showed the most remarkable piece of football courage by going on to win the game 3-2, with a display of football brilliance.

They were now in two finals and the Premiership was in their grasp. Surely they couldn't do it? The games were coming thick and fast. Everyone absolutely vital, nearly all, literally, cup finals but this team seemed to show no sign of being beaten. They literally looked unbeatable.

It was a phenomenal time for Alex Ferguson's young soldiers. They were now a hair's breadth away from immortality. It was so different for Colin's young fighters. They were so close to the edge. The brink of disaster. They didn't show it but the pressure was immense. Games were running out. Achievable points were becoming less. Two types of football pressure, equally harrowing.

Manchester United pressure and Scarborough pressure.

On the following Saturday we played promotion-seeking Cardiff. This brought the visit of one of our ex-managers, Billy Ayre back to the McCain Stadium. Billy was now assistant manager at Cardiff and clearly relishing the challenge of taking this big club back into the Second Division.

Billy had gone through a serious illness and it was great to see him looking so well. Billy was a little thinner but still looking as hard as nails. You crossed Billy at your peril. Billy to all who know him clearly does not experience the cold. On the coldest, frostiest night in the depths of November when every sane person has more layers of clothing on than an Eskimo, Billy would be stood in his ankle socks, shorts and a T shirt, oblivious of the fact it was minus twenty, and even the Polar Bears were wearing their thermals! A hard man but one of life's gentlemen. It was nice to see Billy again.

We played exceptionally well, missing chance after chance, but it was to

We will be back

be five consecutive defeats. They were very sympathetic and expressed that we should have got at least a point. That always washes thin over me. I would rather people said we were crap, they should have banjoed us, but went away without a point. That always feels better to me. That's the way I prefer it.

No doubt it was a great afternoon's work for Billy. To come back to Scarborough a team he both played for and managed and to get the victory Cardiff so much needed. It wasn't so good for everyone connected to Scarborough Football Club. We had played very well. We did create chances but we finished the day without the vital points we so desperately craved for.

The following Monday, as I drove through to York for a meeting, I heard along with the Nation the shocking news of the assassination of Jill Dando. I couldn't believe what I was hearing. I thought I must have misheard the Radio newsreader. Surely not Jill Dando? How could anybody possibly want to kill her? She had been killed by a single bullet to the head, shot outside her Fulham home in broad daylight.

How could it be? Was the World going mad? Quickly theories were formed. It was the work of a spurned lover. It had been carried out by a deranged stalker. It was the work of the Underworld. It was the deed of a Serbian hitman. Whoever was the assassin, left no evidence and the cold-blooded murder of Jill left the Nation in deep shock.

As the police carried out their investigations and the public were asked to recall anything which may assist the police in uncovering the motive and the killer Scarborough Football Club had completed their games for the penultimate month of the Season. We were heading for May.

Manchester United were still in the running for everything. There was even a rumour they may represent Britain in the Eurovision Song Contest! And no doubt if they did they would flipping win that too! Everyone was saying there was no way they could do it. It was too much even for a team of their stature but they were still in there and determined to achieve the impossible.

We finished the month having played forty three games in total and propping up the table again. A million miles away from Manchester United. Was it all over? Was it time to accept Conference football next Season? Could we produce one last surge and escape at the death? Of course we could. There was still nine big points to play for and we could take all nine. Now was the time to carry out the words of the Club's motto, 'No Battle, No Victory.'

14

No battle, no victory

MAY 1999

Sadly, the whole of football was to mourn the loss of one of England's greatest ever leaders. Sir Alf Ramsey had passed away after a long illness. He would be deeply missed. Sir Alf had given the nation its greatest ever footballing achievement back in '66 and now he was gone.

Instantly, the footballing World called for Sir Alf to be remembered for his greatest ever achievement. The new National Stadium should be named after him. Something had to be done for the great man of 1966. His memory must live on. Too often our greatest footballing heroes are laid to rest quietly and forgotten.

Sir Alf had not been involved in the game for so many years. He had been cast aside after failing to take England to the World Cup Finals in 1974 but in the two previous Cups he had only won the Competition and been beaten in the quarter finals in Mexico! He was a man of dignity and a huge influence on English Football and a man who will be sorely missed. Not only by the players who had the good fortune to play under him but an eternally greatful footballing Nation.

There were three games left for us to play. Away to Halifax who were fighting for a play-off place. At home to Plymouth Argyle who were fighting for a play-off place and concluding our league programme with a home fixture to Peterborough United fighting for a play-off place! What a run in! It could

We will be back

not have been more testing. We had three mountains to climb but we were determined to reach the summits! We could reach Everest.

Colin had adapted the approach that training would be short and sharp and that rest would be prevalent. If players weren't fit now they never would be. They needed to recover between matches and be mentally strong. Colin drew on all his footballing experience. He had the nerve. He had to convince his playing squad that they had the nerve too. Everyone was required to have nerves of steel and total self-belief. Nothing less would be good enough.

Halifax were back in the Football League for the first time in six years and were threatening to do what Macclesfield had done the Season before. Come up as Conference champions and go straight up into the Second Division in their first year. They felt capable of achieving this. After all their run-in included a home fixture against sorry Scarborough. This was a home fixture which they felt rightly confident would yield them with three points to take them that stage closer to promotion.

Earlier in the Season they had lead the league, and, if they hadn't sold their prolific goalscorer Geoff Horsfield to Fulham who knows, they might still have been there. They were still in the play-off places and a win against us would give them a good cushion.

In the days leading up to our vitally important encounter with Halifax, Colin arranged for the players to meet in a Posthouse Hotel on the outskirts of Halifax. Here the players would have a pre-match, have time to relax and Colin would gather them together to discuss tactics, roles and responsibilities. It was a big match, everything had to be absolutely spot on. There could be no excuse for bad preparation.

From the Hotel the players would drive to the Shay. There was not to be the luxury of a coach today. This was not the way Colin wanted it to be, but sometimes, too often, finance dictates. They would make their own way to the Stadium. Colin was less than happy about this. Planning and preparation had to be meticulous. The least little interference was unacceptable.

As if this was bad enough, we were informed there was insufficient space for the players to park their cars at the ground. They would have to park elsewhere. This was to say the least a massive game for us and there was the total inconvenience to the players of having to drive themselves to the game, and then hope to find a parking spot. We could do without them worrying about being wheel-clamped !

Fortunately, with a little bit of skullduggery we managed to get everyone parked inside the Stadium grounds and the problem was minimal.

That morning I had taken the Youth Team to Rochdale to play in their final domestic game of the Season. We had asked for an early kick off at Rochdale in order for us to get to the Shay and lend our support. That morning we played particularly well and came away with a much deserved 2-1 win. This was sweet revenge over Rochdale as they had knocked us out of the Youth Cup earlier in the Season. Little did I know the Club was going to finish the day with two, 2-1 away wins!

It was nice to be back at the Shay. Much had changed and it was a very presentable little ground. The May sunshine was very welcoming to the spectators but not so much to the players. It was strength-sapping.

The atmosphere was excellent and the rivalry between the two sets of supporters was warm and friendly to the ears. This was the way a football match should be. Everyone was there to enjoy the day. Cheer their team on and appreciate good football. Halifax supporters prepared their vocal chords for an almighty sound of promotion and our fans prepared themselves to sing themselves hoarse for survival.

As the referee informed the teams it was time to go out Colin sat the players down for a last few words. He told them of the importance of the next week. The need for them to be at their best today and how vital victory was. It was a big game we needed big hearts. He told them to enjoy the occasion. To play with freedom and not to be filled with fear. His last words were, 'We will win'.

The usual rally call was sounded. That moment when players just release that last rush of adrenaline before they take to the field. As they left the dressing room, Colin stood by the door and shook every player's hand as they made their way onto the pitch. The coaching staff shook each others' hands and we followed the players out of the dressing room.

Before the game commenced a minute's silence was to be observed in remembrance of Sir Alf. As the referee blew his whistle to herald the minute of silence I remember praying for Sir Alf to find peace in his rest. I prayed for his grieving family. I prayed to Sir Alf to look down on Scarborough and to smile on our side. Sir Alf help, us to win.

I always pray for the people whose memory is being remembered and often wonder what goes on in the minds of others during that minute of silence. Do they have thoughts? Are they similar to mine? What do they think? It's one of those things I wonder but never discuss!

The minute's silence was impeccable. The Stadium was silent. A mark of respect was observed for a man of honour. As the referee blew his whistle to end the silence the place burst with noise. It was now time to let Sir Alf look down and admire the passion and fervour of football in the English Third Division.

We started like men possessed. Within ten minutes we were two goals to the good and Halifax looked like relegation-fodder. Our football was slick, incisive and effective. We were fighting for our lives and it showed. We were controlling the play and looking comfortable in all areas.

We could not have wished in our wildest dreams for such a brilliant start. We were two goals in front and every time we got the ball we looked like we were going to score. It was just what the doctor ordered. A nice two goal cushion to ease any nerves that were jangling and believe me there were a few of them.

Halifax were at sixes and sevens. Their fans were dumb-struck. Our fans were jubilant. They couldn't get near us and there were more than a fair share of verbals coming from their bench. We were working our socks off in the heat and in charge of affairs.

And then with 10 minutes of the first half left to play our little midfielder Ben Worrall lost possession in our defensive third and it was 2-1. Ben got caught in a momentary lapse of concentration, gave a loose ball away, and paid the price heavily. It had been Halifax's first serious attack on our goal and to be fair they finished it clinically.

Nerves now started to jangle and the flow to our play started to disappear. We went in at half time 2-1 to the good but looking very edgy. We needed time to settle things down and take stock. If anyone had said we would be 2-1 up at half-time we would have gladly accepted that. However, football being football, and Halifax narrowing the gap between us, brought panic stations.

At half time Colin used all his depth of experience to calm and control our side. Their belief had become a little uncertain. The composure had become a touch erratic and action had to be taken. Colin used words of comfort. He told the players he trusted in their ability to win the match. Did they trust in themselves?

There was no need to crumble. Stand strong, stand firm and fight to be first. The players rehydrated, the leaders got stuck into everyone and the quiet men steadied themselves in their own focus and built themselves up for the second forty five. In the corner I heard our goalkeeper tell his defenders that over his dead body were Halifax going to unlock our defence in the next half. A clean sheet from now until full time would mean victory was ours. It was going to be ours.

We will be back

Someone informed the players and staff that it was 0-0 at half time over at Hartlepool. It was not a bad situation for us but it wasn't a time to be concerned with other events in games in our Division. We could only affect our own situation. We would worry about the other results and the consequence at the end of today's fixtures.

The second half it was all hands to the pumps and we rode our luck to get a massive three points. We scrapped and battled and had more than a few scares but we did it. Every man a hero. Every player a winner. The minutes of added on time seemed like hours, even weeks. They seemed like an eternity. Lady luck was with us. Sir Alf was with us.

On the North East coast, Carlisle had stolen a point by all accounts at Hartlepool and remained two points ahead of us with one week of the Season remaining. Their on-loan goalkeeper Jimmy Glass having played a blinder in goal to thwart the Hartlepool attacks. Evidently, he had played out of his skin, foiling attack after attack from the Hartlepool forwards. How we would come to hate that name!

After the game Colin requested all the players to go back to the Posthouse Hotel where we had previously had our pre-match. He wanted everyone to have half an hour together, a light refreshment and a little time to reflect and enjoy the victory. He thanked the players for their efforts and told them to have the Monday off and come back focussed on the vital week ahead.

The players had climbed the first of their three mountains. They were now looking out over the other two. They were formidable challenges but we were all united in our view that we could reach our Everest. The players slowly dispersed from the hotel to make their way back to their homes, everyone having put in a great day at the office!

The 98/99 Season will be remembered for some great and some not so great incidents. Paulo Di Canio's moment of madness, John Hartson's G. B. H. on Eyal Berkovic, Robbie Fowler's stupidity in the Merseyside derby and now in the final week of the Season Ian Wright lost the plot when being sent off. Ian blew a fuse and went in and trashed the referee's room, earning himself a charge of misconduct by the F. A.

The pressures on the modern day footballer are unimaginable. Every step they take, every move they make, 'I'll be watching you' is words from a song that sing so true on the high-profile footballer and they have to cope with and rise above confrontational situations. It is far from easy but do it they must. Young men who must conduct themselves every waking day with the maturity of an experienced Royal.

We will be back

The last week of the Season. Which team was destined for the Conference League? Which team would lose its Football League status? We had two games left. Two massive games. Carlisle had one. Carlisle were on 46 points. We were on 44 points. We would play Plymouth Argyle on Wednesday the 5th. Carlisle would play them on Saturday the 8th.

Plymouth had to beat us to have the chance of getting a play-off place. If we beat them they would go to Carlisle with nothing to play for bar their pride. We would then face Peterborough on the Saturday who had to win to have any chance of a play-off place! Could it have been anymore difficult? I think not.

Talk about pressure. You could cut it with a knife. This was not a place for the feint-hearted. It was the McCain Stadium and the tension was smacking you in the face. Plymouth had travelled up the day before and had come to the Stadium knowing a victory would keep their hopes of the play-offs alive and that defeat would signal the end of their Wembley dreams. That had to be a great psychological boost. It would mean Carlisle would be the team propping up the League on the last Saturday and it would mean they had to win their final game. Anything less would be tragic to Carlisle.

We knew that our destiny was still in our hands. If we won, we would go one point ahead of Carlisle going into the final game of the Season. They would then have to win their final game. Anything less would be fantastic for Scarborough. If we drew or lost then we would have to depend on Carlisle dropping points on the last Saturday. It was imperative we controlled our own destiny on Saturday the 8th May!

Many loyal Plymouth fans had made the long journey up to the Theatre of Chips. They were in good heart, knowing that a win would put their team in strong contention for the play-offs, knowing that their support was so welcome to their team. The away stand was filled with faithful fans in green and white, singing their songs of support, rallying their team for another big effort and willing them to give the travelling fans the opportunity of contesting a play-off place. And provide them, like us at this stage last Season, of a possible trip to Wembley.

Scarborough fans were again not out in great numbers. We were fighting for our lives and there was a smell of apathy around the town. Everyone knows the value of a successful football club. Everyone knows the value of belonging to the Football League but yet here we were in possibly our penultimate game in the Football League and not too many Scarborians seemed to really care.

As Winston Churchill said 'You're country needs you'. We needed fans

We will be back

in the trenches to give us the assistance that a loud, vocal home support can give. A noise and the encouragement to knock over the strongest resisting army. The support to ensure we got everything we could get at home. It wasn't to be. We had to stand alone and fight to keep the town in the Football League. To keep Scarborough where it belongs.

Again, before the match started Scarborough Football Club was to have a minute's silence for Sir Alf Ramsey. Again I prayed to Sir Alf and his family. I asked Sir Alf to stick with us tonight and twinkle his eye on Scarborough. For him to rest in peace and I thanked him for giving English football its finest hour. Not a sound was heard as the people remembered. One more time. Come on Sir Alf stick with us!

We started well and got better as the game progressed. We moved the ball with confidence, kept our shape and discipline and pegged Plymouth back into their own half for long periods. We were playing like a side pushing for promotion, not a side fighting to avoid relegation. We were on top and it was only a matter of time before we scored. We did. A clever free-kick taken by our on-loan midfielder Nathan Jones put Darren Roberts in down the left hand side and deadly Darren rifled the opening goal into the bottom corner of the net.

A great goal and much deserved. However, we continued to create chance after chance, hitting the woodwork and forcing excellent saves from the visiting 'keeper. Was it going to be one of those nights when after dictating much of the play the whole thing would rebound in our faces? Not tonight.

Late in the second half, after incessant pressure, Chris Tate released the tension by firing in our second and followed that up moments later with a third goal. What a win. What a performance. We had played Plymouth off the park. It could have easily been, without exaggeration, six or seven. We had done it, we were second bottom of the table going into the final Saturday. If we could win we stayed up. If we drew and Carlisle drew we stayed up. If we lost and Carlisle drew we stayed up. If we drew and Carlisle won... No, it couldn't happen. No way!

If only we had played the way we had played against Plymouth more often during the course of the Season we certainly would not have the worry of relegation hanging over us, we would more likely have had the excitement of perhaps finishing as champions of the league. The performance was that good. Slick, stylish and sure.

Plymouth players knew they had blown their big chance. A play-off place was not to be. They were as you can imagine, devastated. But, they were noble in defeat. They accepted they were very much second best on the night and that we more than deserved our three goal victory. They wished us every chance of survival and re-assured us that they would give everything they had against Carlisle on Saturday. We thanked them and hoped that they could find a big performance to defeat the Cumbrians.

It had been a marvellous exhibition of football. We had climbed the second summit. One more and we would be safe. We had pulled ourselves out of the mire and given ourselves every opportunity to remain in the Football League. We were all exhausted by the events of the night. Mentally and emotionally drained.

The players had the next day off. They were to report in on the Friday for a light session before the big one on the Saturday. Nobody was carrying any injuries. It was what they needed, rest, relaxation and recovery. How much relaxation I'm not sure. They had a couple of days before the most important game in the history of Scarborough Football Club. For some, it must have been very tense and nerve-racking.

As we wrestled with relegation, the Premiership title was drawing itself closer to Manchester. History could be made by both Clubs, Manchester United and Scarborough. Both Clubs could go down in their Clubs' history. United for the right reasons. Scarborough for the wrong.

The lead up to the Saturday was relaxed around the Stadium. We were expecting a bumper crowd. The Administration staff had been inundated by callers enquiring about prices, if it was all-ticket and wishing us all the best. The Club had been strictly informed that the game must start on time and that security was paramount. There could be no delays, nothing to delay the start or finish of the game. Any indiscretions could result in severe action from the footballing hierarchy.

Extra security and policing were put in place to meet the strong sanctions laid down by the governing bodies. Every precaution was taken by the Club to guarantee punctuality. There would be no delays. The game would commence and cease on time. There would be no excuse for delays. Prior to the match or during the match.

I remember thinking before the game started about Sir Alf. I wanted another minute's silence. He had been with us in our previous two matches, but I knew we couldn't go on having a minute's silence for Sir Alf forever! We had to do it without Sir Alf today.

Superstition can be an over-powering thing in the minds of footballers and all involved in football. And superstition was around the McCain Stadium that day. People had to follow the exact same ritual they had followed

We will be back

in the lead up to the previous two games. To the previous two victories. Same tie. Same underpants. Same seats. You name it, it had to be the same. Nothing could be altered or it could have tragic consequences. Marriages could be terminated if spouses caused doubt in the minds of their partners!

I had spoken with a fan during the week. A fan who had supported us through thick and thin. Through good and bad. A fan who was always there. But he would not be there on Saturday! He had for some unavoidable reason missed the Plymouth game. It must have been for something like a family bereavement to keep him away. But absent he was. And, consequently, superstition took hold. He would not go. He felt his absence had given us victory over Plymouth and his absence on Saturday would ensure another Scarborough victory.

It was the biggest game the Club had faced. He had seen all the other big games in the years previous, but he definitely would not see us against Peterborough. What a sacrifice for the sake of his team. I'm sure there must have been hundreds of other similar stories of superstition. Everyone scared to breathe in case it affected our chances of survival!

Coaching staff during the Peterborough game. 8 May 1999

We will be back

As I left to go to the Stadium I remember spotting a lone Magpie on the way. To some this usually signifies sorrow. I try to keep superstition out of my life, but sometimes it inextricably creeps in. I didn't know whether to pretend I hadn't seen it or re-assure myself that I had saw a solo Magpie the week before as we made our way to Rochdale, and on that occasion we had our two away victories. Yes I'm sure I did!

I remember thinking as I approached the Stadium about Manchester United. How they were on the verge of an incredible piece of footballing history. They were set up to be remembered by so many for so many years to come for their unbelievable success. And thinking were we going to be remembered by so few for our failures in the Season 1998/1999?

The ten minute journey into the Stadium from my home had me 'butterflying' from thought to thought. My mind was everywhere. Superstition, prayers, forecast, spinning all over the place. The journey seemed to take a second. I had no sooner set off from my home to me turning up into Lismore Road and into the car park.

That leads me onto another story. Getting your car parked at the McCain Stadium is like swimming the channel in hob-nailed boots. Or getting a drink out of a Scotsman, especially this Scotsman! It's very difficult to do! You have to use great stealth to weasel your way past the Gestapo, or as some affectionately call them, the stewards. It doesn't matter who you are, if your name is not down on their list and there is no designated space for you, you certainly don't get in.

The car park, on a good day, at the McCain Stadium can just about take three cars, a push bike and a pogo stick. As you can imagine today it was going to have to try to accommodate a little extra. I, being a mere youth team manager had not been designated a space. I always relished such challenges. Could I inveigle my way past Ivan the Terrible on the gate? Could I acquire one of the precious parking lots reserved for the almighty?

As I drove towards Ivan, my plan back-fired big time. I was going to adopt the identity of one of our directors. When asked my name I gave him the name of one of the almighty and was just about to drive on through when a big fist appeared in front of the windscreen. 'Who did you say you are, Sir?' I repeated the name of the Director. 'I don't think so', he groaned.' He is already in the ground,Sir'. Preposterous I mumbled, I will find out who this impostor is and have him ejected I said, as I reversed and ended up parked in the B&Q Car Park! About two bus journeys away from the ground!

On a normal Saturday the hour before a game at the McCain Stadium sheds about as much life as is found in a morgue. It's not like Anfield here,

113

We will be back

its more like a cemetery. Its not until the last fifteen minutes before kick off that life can be found. Even then, it's sometimes difficult to find!

On this Saturday, unlike every Saturday before, the crowds were pouring down Seamer Road. There was much congestion outside. This was almost like a real football match. This was the real McCoy. If we were not careful we might find ourselves with over ten people in the queue waiting to gain admission! Regardless of any possible delay, referee Roy Pearson insisted the game would start on time.

The late arrivers would not be appeased. They either missed the start of the game or they would be locked outside. Many of them sauntered down Seamer Road at their normal time of arrival expecting to waltz through the turnstiles and take their place just as the opening whistle blew.

Today, they would find complications and some of our most loyal supporters might not even see this game which would decide whether it was Football League or Conference next Season. As much as they appealed outside for leniency their words of mercy fell on deaf ears. This was the most important game in the history of Scarborough Football Club. They had supported us through thick and thin and they were so needed today. Their admission was refused. They had to be satisfied with watching the game from the adjoining local school.

Our game started and finished on time and the impossible happened. Oh how it happened.

Darren Roberts after missing a glorious opportunity to put us 2-1 up against Peterborough. 8 May 1999

15

The end of an era

We finished the 1998/1999 Season in 24th place. We were the bottom Club in the Nationwide League Third Division. We would make way for the Conference Champions Cheltenham and we would take their place in the Conference next Season. It was heart-rendering. We were down. After months of complete trust that we would survive we had to accept the reality that we were relegated.

We had drawn our final game and Carlisle did the unmentionable and won their last game. We took one point. They took three. They finished one, miserly point above us. It was the most sickening blow. A worse scenario I cannot conceive.

The bitter pill we had to swallow became even more bitter in the days ahead. Carlisle had survived, good luck to them. But, for me there were questions that had to be asked. Surely, certain incidents had to be examined and an explanation given.

What had caused that mammoth period of time when we found ourselves waiting endlessly for the Carlisle score to be relayed to us? Why had their game finished so long after our game? If there was this strict instruction laid down categorically by the governing bodies that games MUST start and finish on time, what had caused this discrepancy in time?

Carlisle had sold their 'keeper on deadline day to Blackpool. They took a young 'keeper on loan from Derby. He was recalled after deadline day as Derby had a goalkeeping crisis!

We will be back

They took on loan Jimmy Glass from Swindon. What a signing he turned out to be. He would go down as one of Carlisle's great heroes in years to come. He would go down as one of Scarborough's biggest ever nightmares forevermore.

Carlisle could do this under Regulation 37.4 in the Football League Regulations. It said that Clubs are reminded that this Season the deadline for the registration of players falls on Thursday the 25th March, 1999 at 5.00 p.m. Players registered after this date will only be eligible to play in League or Cup matches for which permission is granted by the Board of Directors.

For your information, the Board allow these players to play only in matches which do not have a bearing on promotion or relegation issues.

Any club signing a player after the deadline must apply to the League for permission to play the player in any League organised match.

Regulation 37.5 states that a club may register a short term loan transfer of a recognised goalkeeper after the deadline, subject to all the other recognised professional goalkeepers at the club being declared unfit to play in that match by an independent medical practitioner.

Our Club Solicitors looked into these Regulations and informed us that Carlisle were perfectly within their rights to do this. I couldn't believe the substance of these two Regulations. It seemed beyond belief.

My argument was that if this was acceptable, next Season, as preposterous as it seemed, this crazy scenario could arise. York City are going into the last game of the Season. They need three points to survive. Deadline day has passed. Their goalkeeper has been recently having a nightmare. So, conveniently, on the advice of his team manager, he develops a big back problem and the Club doctor registers him unfit to play. It's a slipped disc!

The Club does not have another 'keeper on their books so they have to get special dispensation to loan another 'keeper, according to the Football League Regulations. Not just any 'keeper. They ring Arsene Wenger at Arsenal and ask to borrow David Seaman. David comes, plays out of his skin and keeps a clean sheet and, voila, York stay up. Crazy, but possible!

During the Carlisle v Plymouth match we were informed there were two pitch invasions. Consequently, Carlisle's match finished some time after our match. Carlisle had a period of time when they knew the Scarborough score and knew they had to win. Allegedly, their P. A. announcer ensured every man and his dog knew, especially the Carlisle players and their supporters. They won in that period of time! This it seems was the reason for the massive period of time that elapsed between the conclusion of our game and the finish of their game with Plymouth.

In previous experiences of such incidents severe action was taken. I have nothing against Carlisle but if action isn't seen to be taken then a very serious precedent could be set. I seem to remember Brighton in recent years involved in a very similar situation and subsequently finding themselves having points deducted for their fans' actions!

Now, take this second crazy scenario. Next year it is the turn of Darlington and Hartlepool to take the place of Scarborough and Carlisle. One is going to go down. One is going to stay up, depending on their results on the last Saturday of the Season.

The Darlington fans recall what happened last Season at Carlisle and think they will follow suit. They premeditatingly decide that, if required, there will be a pitch invasion. Their game will be stopped, if necessary, and delayed for a lengthy period of time. The Hartlepool game will finish on time and they will give their team a period of time to determine their outcome. This surely cannot be allowed to happen. There surely must be very strong action taken to ensure it does not occur again.

As far as I'm aware nothing has happened. No action has been taken against Carlisle by the Footballing authorities and yes it could happen again next year. This seems grossly unfair and totally senseless. Action should be seen to be taken.

There are other incidents which have come to light which are not fact so therefore have to be kept within the confines of our Club but they are incidents which leave a bit of a nasty taste in the mouth. And make the acceptance of our relegation more difficult to take.

We are one of the minnows of football. Minnows cannot make a big splash so we will go without raising a ripple. If it had been one of the big fish who had suffered our plight I just wonder if it would have been swept under the carpet as our situation appears to have been! I think not.

We have to live with reality and accept our fate. 1998/1999 Season was the Season that cost us our Football League status. We will be going into the Millennium as a Nationwide Conference side. A very sad fact of life for everyone connected to Scarborough Football Club.

Scarborough Football Club had come into the Football League in 1987/1988, the first team to gain automatic promotion from the

We will be back

Vauxhall Conference League. We had come in on the back of a phenomenal late run to pip Barnet at the post. Their entry into the league would come later. That magnificent achievement still burns bright in the memory of so many of our supporters.

We had spent 11 glorious Seasons in the Football League. There was no steady rise or fall, it was like a rollercoaster ride. We had been at both ends of the table. We were for so long at the top end of the table in our last but one Season in the Football League. We were so long rooted to the bottom end of the table in our final year.

What had brought about the massive transformation in the Club's fortunes between the 1997/1998 Season and the 1998/1999 Season?

Why had the Club come so close to Second Division status the previous Season and this Season been demoted out of the Football League. We had finished our penultimate Season looking like a strong and formidable little Club that was heading in the right direction. Then calamity struck. Why?

Football is a game of opinions, that is the beauty and appeal of the game and many opinions have been given and many more will be offered.' It was Wadsworth's fault. He should have gone long before he did.'

'It was Anton Johnson's fault. He should never have been allowed anywhere near the McCain Stadium'. 'He has taken this Club into the Nationwide Conference'.

'It was John Russell to blame. He should have made more money available for players. If he had dug deeper into his pocket we would still be playing in the Football League next Season.'

'It was the players' fault. They weren't good enough. They didn't care and they were only interested in receiving their pay cheques. That's the trouble with our players their hearts aren't in the Club. As long as they receive their big salaries they don't care which League we play in.'

'We changed the manager too many times in such a short space of time. There was no stability. The players didn't get the continuity of one manager's voice long enough to draw breathe let alone understand tactics and team strategies'. 'How could we expect to stay up with all the chopping and changing'.

'It was the fans' fault. If they had turned up in numbers more often we would have stayed up. If they had heeded all the pleas from the Club in our Season of need we would never have gone down. Too many of them didn't care enough. There is too much apathy in the town towards the Club. This town doesn't deserve a Football League Club'.

Everyone will have and give their opinions. Many will give different views. All will be given honestly. Some will be given by people who have no idea what they are talking about. They've never been, never set foot inside the McCain Stadium, but they know the reason for our demise.

It doesn't matter, Scarborough Football Club is down. That is the fact of the matter. We, as a Club, must all accept a piece of the responsibility. No single incident or single person caused our relegation. It was a conglomeration of events but the bottom line is we didn't win sufficient games. We didn't accumulate adequate points. We finished the Season with the least points and therefore we will find ourselves playing Conference football next Season.

Through adversity must rise strength. The future is where we must look now. What has happened cannot be undone. The Club must remain solid and focussed. It is a time for strong character and positive direction. We must stick together and ensure brighter tomorrows.

Regularly I have flashbacks of that fateful day and regularly I relive those dreadful moments. It was a living nightmare. But from the most horrible experiences sometimes strengths are found.

However, I would not wish it on my worst footballing enemy. That day will be etched in my memory forever.

I looked round our dressing room and I witnessed the feelings and emotions of many grown men. I looked around the ground and I saw the faces of many weeping fans. I saw the tears flow from many of our young players who were connected to the Club and I learned that the future of the Club lay in their hands.

We had put together a Youth Policy which was now starting to bear fruit. It has to be kept in place. It has to be allowed to mature. It would be so easy to walk away and let the whole thing die a death. There is absolutely no way that will be allowed to happen. There are too many totally committed people who would let that happen over their dead bodies.

The letters, faxes and telephone calls we received from other Football League Clubs expressing their commiserations and sadness that we would no longer be with them next Season was very touching and sincere. We had made so many friends during our time in the league and it was very gratifying to know from so many, how much they cared about our plight.

We will be back

Much blood, sweat and tears have been shed much more will be given. As long as the faithful live and breathe. As long as they have something to give Scarborough Football Club will survive and strive to renew its Football League status. We are a proud Club who have come a long way. Determination, drive, desire and dedication will always be found around the McCain Stadium. There are too many committed people who want to take the Club back where it belongs and in the words of our Chairman to the fans on that most awful Saturday in May:

'WE WILL BE BACK !'